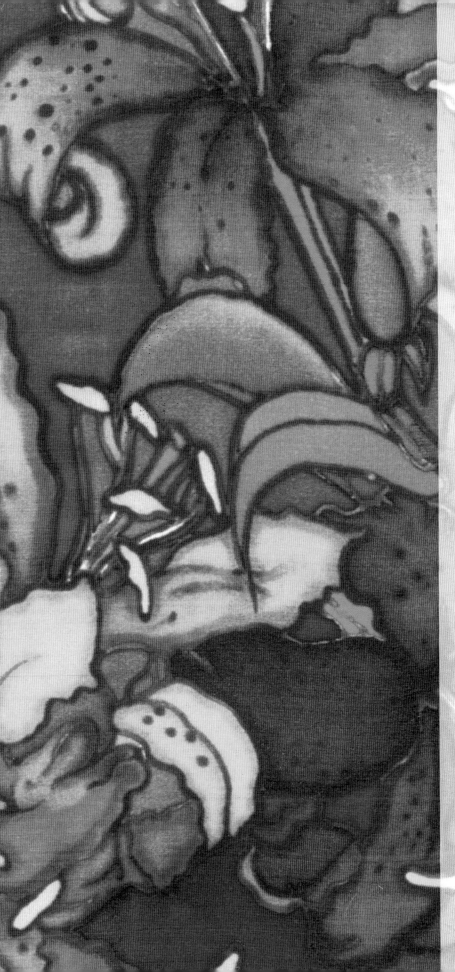

Painting Flowers on Silk

For my parents

Painting Flowers on Silk

Mandy Southan

SEARCH PRESS

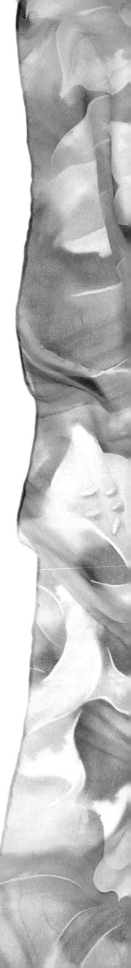

First published in Great Britain 2000

Search Press Limited
Wellwood, North Farm Road,
Tunbridge Wells, Kent TN2 3DR

Text copyright © Mandy Southan 2000

Photographs by Search Press Studios
Photographs and design copyright © Search Press Ltd. 2000

ISBN 0 85532 901 7

The Publishers and author can accept no responsibility for any consequences arising from the information, advice or instructions given in this publication.

Readers are permitted to reproduce any of the items/patterns in this book for their personal use, or for the purposes of selling for charity, free of charge and without the prior permission of the Publishers. Any use of the items/patterns for commercial purposes is not permitted without the prior permission of the Publishers.

Suppliers

If you have difficulty in obtaining any of the materials and equipment mentioned in this book, then please visit the Search Press website for details of suppliers:
www.searchpress.com

Alternatively, you can write to the Publishers at the address above, for a current list of stockists, which includes firms who operate a mail-order service.

Publishers' note

All the step-by-step photographs in this book feature the author, Mandy Southan, demonstrating how to paint flowers on silk. No models have been used.

Colour separation by Graphics '91 Pte Ltd, Singapore
Printed in Spain by Elkar S. Coop. Bilbao 48012

Special thanks to my husband, Ian, and my children, Jenny, Ben and Jack, for their love and patience while I have been immersed in flowers and silk over the past year.

I would also like to thank everyone at Search Press, especially Chantal Roser for her sensitive and skilful editing, Julie Wood for her imaginative design work, and Lotti de la Bédoyère for her excellent photography – it has been a pleasure working with them.

Thank you also to all my students who constantly refire my enthusiasm for painting and teaching.

Lastly, I would like to thank all my family and friends for the happiness they have given me.

Page 1 Tiger lilies
The violet outlines in this painting are made by mixing violet dye with thickener (epaississant) – this is not a true resist but it is effective as long as you do not make the painting too wet!

Pages 2–3 Anemones
These anemones are painted with dyes mixed with thickener to prevent the colours from spreading.

Pages 4–5 Amaryllis scarf
This pretty silk georgette scarf is painted using wax to partially define the amaryllis flowers, and diffusing medium to stripe the petals and leaves.

Contents

Introduction

When I was asked to write a book on painting flowers on silk, I knew it would be a wonderful project to work on. I adore all flowers – cultivated, wild and exotic – and I also love painting on silk, so the chance to combine my interests was irresistible!

I am constantly amazed by the complexity of design in nature, and I find the diversity of colours and shapes in flowers an endless source of inspiration for my paintings and textile designs. Silk is a wonderful surface to work on, and a number of intriguing techniques can be used to achieve unusual effects, providing new possibilities for flower painters. I work with steam-fix silk dyes as they are easy to use and the colours are very pure, making it easy to achieve clear and vibrant flowers.

In this book I have painted some of my favourite flowers as step-by-step projects using a variety of techniques to illustrate the breadth and diversity of the medium. I have included designs so you can copy the projects, or you may prefer to use the methods and ideas shown to paint your own flowers. Remember, there is no 'one way' or 'right way' to paint flowers. You can use any of the techniques covered in this book, and each will achieve completely different results. Think about what you want to express in your painting before you start, then consider which technique might best convey what you feel about the flower or flowers you have chosen.

All the projects can be painted on a 50 x 50cm (19½ x 19½in) frame (there will be a little surplus silk around some designs), or you can use an adjustable frame to get the exact inside measurement, as given for each project. You can also adapt the projects for larger pieces if you like!

I have included a section on colour mixing, as I am aware that many people find this difficult. All the colours in the projects are mixed from six basic colours (see page 12). The basic colours required for each project are given in the *You Will Need* lists.

I have taught painting on silk for many years, and I have found that the majority of my students love painting flowers. Beginners are fascinated to discover how the dyes spread and fill the spaces outlined with resists, and are excited by the wonderful colours they can mix. As confidence and experience grow, students try other techniques, and start to experiment further, allowing the medium to offer its own unique magic.

If you have no artistic experience, do not be deterred – you will be amazed by what you can achieve very quickly. If you are already an experienced flower painter, but are used to working on paper, you will probably be captivated when you try painting flowers on silk. Even if you already paint flowers on silk, I am sure this book will give you some new ideas. Whatever your level of artistic ability, I hope the following pages will add a little fertiliser to your creative soil!

French flowers

French flower markets are a delight! Bunches of mixed flowers are arranged in wonderful combinations of colours. These flowers were painted freely directly on to dry silk. A little clear gutta was used to define the centres of the daisies.

Materials

A comprehensive selection of materials is featured in this section, but you do not need all this to begin silk painting – all you need is a frame, a piece of silk, a brush and a few basic colours. A list of materials required accompanies each project, but in addition you will need jars of clean water, paper towelling, palettes and droppers.

Silk

Different types are available for painting, and each produces different results. I have specified which silk I have used for each project.

Steam-fix silk dyes

These are very versatile and easy to work with. The colours are vibrant and can be manipulated on the silk to achieve beautiful textural effects unique to silk painting.

Droppers

These are used for transferring dyes from bottles to a palette.

Discharge dyes and illuminants

These are special dyes used in the discharge technique. Dyes which can be bleached out of the silk with a reducing agent (discharge salt) are 'dischargeable'. Dyes which are unaffected by a reducing agent are called 'illuminants'. They are used to replace a discharged area with another colour.

Brushes

Foam, mop, flat and round brushes are all useful. You will need a variety of sizes. Soft-haired, springy brushes with good points are easiest to work with. Brushes should be washed in warm water with a little soap to remove surplus dye from under the ferrule. Rinse and dry them carefully, reshaping the hairs into a point.

Palette

An ice cube tray makes an excellent palette, and a porcelain or plastic watercolour palette can also be used. If you are working on large pieces, use a palette with deep wells so that it will hold plenty of dye, or use small jars.

Resists and applicators

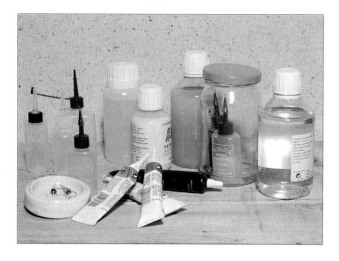

Clear water-based gutta is available in tubes and jars. Water-based gutta is washed out of the silk after fixing. It forms a reasonable resist but will not stand up to repeated overpainting.

Clear spirit-based gutta is a liquid latex rubber which forms an excellent resist. Fine lines can be left in the silk or removed after fixing by dry-cleaning or by rinsing in white spirit.

Spirit-based gutta can be stored in a **screw-top jar** containing a little **white spirit** to stop it evaporating and thickening.

Essence 'F' is a spirit sold with spirit-based gutta to thin it to the correct consistency – that of runny honey.

Coloured guttas and **metallic outliners** are available in many different colours. You can buy them in tubes or jars.

You can transfer gutta into a **gutta bottle** fitted with a **gutta nib**. Gutta nibs come in different widths – fine ones for fine line work, and larger ones for metallic outliners and broad outlines.

Gutta wire is used to seal the fine spout of the gutta nib when not in use. It prevents the gutta from drying and blocking the nib. It is not stiff enough to use to unblock a spout – you should use a fine needle instead.

Special effect materials

Etching gel is a chemical which dissolves cellulose. It is used on viscose/silk mixes such as velvet to create a devoré design. It 'burns out' the viscose pile whilst leaving the silk backing intact.

Anti-spread medium is used to treat the silk so that the dyes will not spread when they are applied. You can also make your own anti-spread by mixing thickener with water.

Diffusing medium is a levelling agent which can be mixed with the dyes to help them spread and blend evenly on the silk. It can also be used instead of water to create tints of colours. It can be applied over painted areas to create interesting marks and textures.

Coarse salt such as rock or sea salt will make bold patterns when sprinkled on to damp painted silk. **Fine salt** makes more delicate patterns.

Discharge salt is a reducing agent which bleaches out colour.

Thickener can be mixed with dyes or discharge salt and illuminants to prevent the colours from spreading. It can also be mixed with a little dye and used as a coloured water-based gutta, or mixed with water to treat the silk to produce an anti-spread surface.

Wax equipment

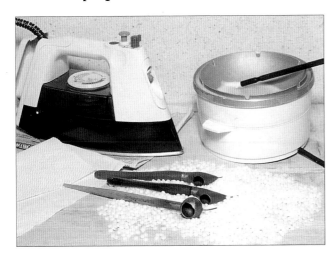

An **electric wax pot** is used to melt wax. It is thermostatically controlled to keep the melted wax at the correct temperature.

General purpose **batik wax granules** are melted down in the wax pot and used as a resist. They can be purchased from craft shops and silk painting and candle maker's suppliers. Cheaper paraffin wax can also be used.

Tjantings are brass- or copper-bowled Javanese tools with fine spouts. They are used to draw the melted wax on to the silk.

A natural-haired **brush** is used to paint on the melted wax.

An **iron** is used for ironing out wax and for removing creases from finished pieces. Protect your ironing board with a clean cotton cloth or newspaper.

Old newspapers or clean newsprint are used when ironing out wax. Do not use fresh newspapers, as these can transfer ink to the silk.

Paper towelling is used for wiping brushes and removing surplus dye from waxed areas.

Other materials

Silk is pinned to a **frame** to prevent it from touching your work surface as you paint it. Wooden and plastic ones are available in various adjustable designs. The frame needs to be the size of the piece of silk you are working on.

Three-point silk pins or **stenter pins** and **rubber bands** are used to attach silk to the frame. The latter are particularly useful for pinning silk with pre-rolled edges and for silk velvet. You should re-tension the silk as necessary as you are working, so that the dye dries evenly.

Designs can be raised under the silk on a **board**, and protected with **polythene**.

You can draw on to silk with an **autofade marker**. The lines will fade automatically after a few hours or when dye or water is applied. A **soft graphite or charcoal pencil** can also be used for drawing on to the silk – use lightly, as heavy line work will show up in the finished painting.

A **water mister** is used for damping the silk.

Silk can be cut with **scissors** or nicked and then torn on the grain.

Brushes should be rinsed in a **water jar**. Have at least two jars of water beside you as you work and keep one clean for mixing colours.

A **hairdryer** is used to dry dye and gutta.

Plastic gloves should be worn to protect hands from dye stains and chemicals.

Using colour

Good colour mixing is important when painting flowers, perhaps more so than for any other subject. There is nothing more frustrating than trying to capture the beautiful violet of a pansy but only managing to mix a dirty brown or grey!

For many painters, however, colour mixing can be a confusing business. The most important thing is to select the correct colours to start with and to be able to identify the difference between them.

<table>
<tr><td>

— TIP —

You can make tints by adding water or diffusing medium to a colour.

</td></tr>
</table>

Basic colours

I use a small range of six basic colours: orangey yellow, greeny yellow, greeny blue, violety blue, violety red and orangey red. These can be intermixed to produce a virtually endless range of colours.

All the projects in this book list only the basic blues, reds and yellows needed, and from these you will need to mix up the other colours before you begin the project.

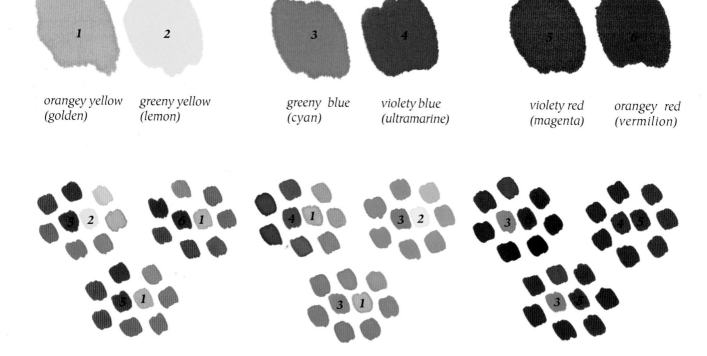

orangey yellow (golden)
greeny yellow (lemon)
greeny blue (cyan)
violety blue (ultramarine)
violety red (magenta)
orangey red (vermilion)

Yellows and reds can be mixed together to make oranges

Yellows and blues can be mixed together to make greens

Blues and reds can be mixed together to make violets

Complementary colours

When the colours of the spectrum are arranged in a circle (a colour wheel) the complementary colours are found opposite each other: oranges and blues; greens and reds; violets and yellows. These complementary 'pairs' of colours are very important in painting and can be used to create many different effects (see pages 14–15).

oranges and blues   *greens and reds*   *violets and yellows*

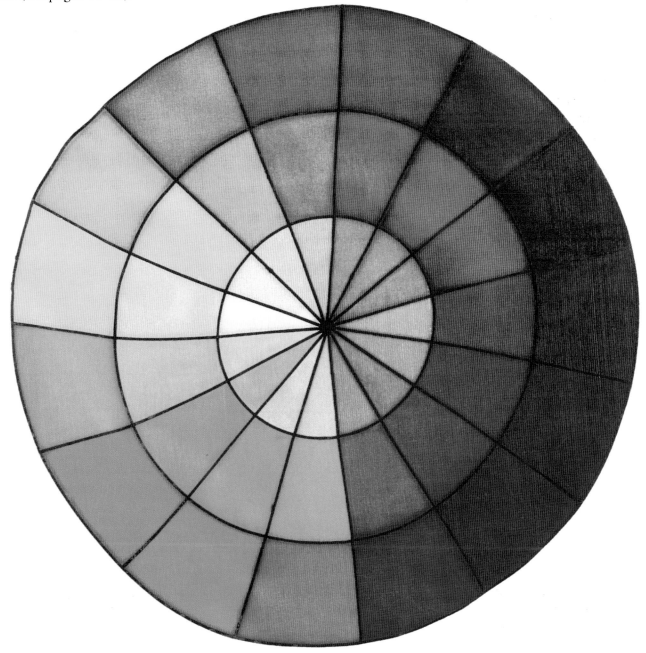

Subtle colours

If you mix complementary colours together you get wonderful ranges of browns, greys and even blacks! If you want to subdue or darken a colour, mix in its complementary colour. Try introducing a tiny bit at a time until you get the colour you want. Never use black – this simply deadens the colour.

Enhancing colours

If you paint complementary colours next to each other, they tend to enhance each other.

Jumping colours

If you make the tones of the complementary pair the same (so that neither one appears darker than the other when you look at them through half-closed eyes), they 'jump' against each other and can be used to create startling effects.

Petunias

The full vibrancy of silk dye colours only becomes apparent after steaming. Some pinks can become very strong, as these petunias show. It is always a good idea to test your colours before you use them for your final paintings – you will usually be delighted by the brilliance of the colours, but sometimes a subtle pink can turn into a shocking one!

16

Fixing dyes

When you have completed your painting, the dyes need to be steam-fixed so that they become colour-fast. Painted silk looks beautiful after steaming; the colours often become brighter and more intense, and the full sheen of the silk is restored. Even if you do not intend to wash your painting, it should still be fixed to make it light-fast.

Fixing involves wrapping the painted silk in cotton cloth or paper to prevent it from smudging, then exposing it to plenty of steam so that the dyes are able to combine with the silk fibres. Boiling when dip-dyeing serves the same purpose. Steaming with a steam iron is not sufficient to fix the dyes properly.

The fixing process is very simple and can be done in several different ways. The demonstration on page 18 shows how to steam-fix in a bamboo steamer. Follow the procedure carefully to avoid mishaps. Remember you want plenty of steam – not water – to get into your roll of painted silk. Keep everything dry in preparation and do not put too much water into the pan as it can bubble up and splash the silk. Always keep silk steaming equipment separate from that used for food.

After steaming, rinse the silk in cold running water to remove any excess dye. If you have used clear water-based gutta, you then need to soak the silk for a few minutes in warm water to remove all traces of the gutta. Towel dry or short spin, then iron it while still damp to remove the creases and restore the sheen of the silk.

A Chinese bamboo steamer fitted over a saucepan makes a very effective and inexpensive steamer. It is better than a metal one because it does not build up condensation. Allow the steamer to dry thoroughly between steamings as it can become saturated. Steam for approximately 1–2 hours, depending on the weight of the silk.

A pressure cooker shortens the steaming time considerably (down to approximately ten minutes). Be careful not to block the safety valve with too large a bundle. Fill with about 2.5cm (1in) of water and turn the heat down low when it has reached pressure to prevent it from boiling dry.

If you are painting lots of silk, a professional steamer is a good investment. You can steam large paintings and long lengths of silk in it. There are several different types – stove-top steamers are laid horizontally across a cooker, and the upright model shown here has a built-in electric element. Steam for approximately two hours, depending on the weight of the silk.

1. Cut a piece of clean, dry cloth (thin cotton sheeting is ideal) approximately 10cm (4in) bigger all round than the piece of silk that you want to steam. Lay the silk flat in the middle of the cloth and smooth out any creases. Roll up the cloth and silk loosely.

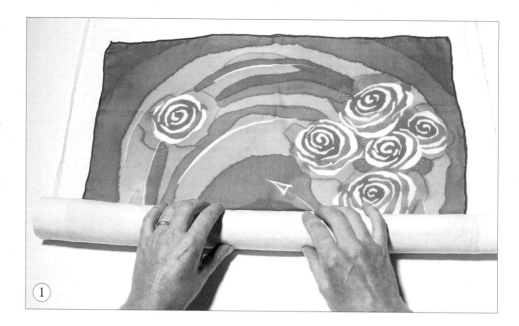

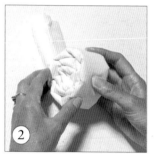

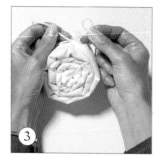

2. Coil the roll to make a snail-like bundle.

3. Secure the bundle with string. Tuck in the loose ends of the string to make a neat package.

4. Cut four circles of kitchen foil to fit inside the steamer. Place two circles in the bottom of the steamer, put the bundle on top, and then place the remaining two circles of foil on top of the bundle. Smooth down the foil over the sides of the bundle to make an umbrella shape – this will prevent condensation from dripping on to the bundle.

5. Fill a saucepan one-third full of boiling water. Place the steamer on top of the saucepan then place the lid on the steamer. Steam for 1–2 hours depending on the size of the silk. If you have to top up the water level during this time, use boiling water. When the silk is steamed, unwrap it and rinse it in cold running water to remove any dye residue.

How to start

There are lots of different ways of approaching flower painting on silk. Here are just some of them!

Working from designs

If you have no artistic experience or lack confidence in your creative abilities, you can use the linear designs in this book or work from tracings of photographs. You can transfer the designs on to silk using a soft graphite pencil, an autofade marker, gutta or outliner. If you trace from a photograph, remember that you need not copy it exactly as it is. The design may be improved by adding an extra flower, or leaving out a leaf! Use a photocopier to enlarge to the size you want. You can then enjoy the painting process without the anxiety of feeling you have to be able to draw first!

Working from photographs

Some flower painters like to work from photographs because flowers move and change as you paint them, and sometimes wither before the painting is finished. Photographs can also provide plenty of inspiration during the winter months, when there are not so many flowers around to paint. You can find beautiful photographs in gardening books and flower catalogues, or better still, take your own. This way you will have had the chance to study the real flowers and therefore have a deeper understanding of their growth and structure.

Working from real flowers

I prefer to work from real flowers. Before I start a painting, I make graphite pencil drawings in line and tone, or I use coloured pencils – this helps me to understand each flower's form and structure. Through drawing, I begin to simplify and clarify what I want to say about the flowers in my painting. I try to capture the 'essence' of each flower.

Before beginning to draw, it is a good idea to study the flower closely for a few minutes. Turn it round and examine the formation of the petals, the way the leaves grow out of the stem, how the buds open – all the details unique to that flower. When you feel you are beginning to understand it, make a simple line drawing on a large sheet of paper. Follow the edges of the flower,

stem and leaves. As you draw, keep your eyes almost continuously on the flower, not on the paper. Let your eyes move slowly around the edges of the plant, and as they do, let your hand holding the pencil trace the contours of the plant as you see them. Do not lift the pencil off the paper, and try to resist taking your eyes off the plant to check what you are drawing. A quick glance is alright from time to time, just to make sure you are still on the paper and not drawing all over the table! It is surprising how easy and absorbing this kind of drawing is, and how expressive the results are.

Now make a second drawing. This time, look a little more often at the paper. As you draw, compare shapes and relationships between one thing and another. Look at the spaces between the leaves and petals, for example. These are known as 'negative shapes'. Try to see them as actual shapes and draw these abstract shapes rather than the plant itself. In this way, your drawings will become much more accurate.

The drawings you make can be traced directly on to the silk if you wish, or used as a valuable reference for your painting.

Drawing directly on to silk

As your confidence and observational skills increase, you can sketch freely and loosely directly on to silk using an autofade marker and then apply resists over selected sketch lines if you wish; or you can draw directly on to the silk using resists. The latter requires careful observation because incorrect lines cannot easily be removed. Drawings made using either of these methods have a freshness and immediacy which traced drawings can lose.

TIPS

If you have drawn on the silk with an autofade marker, you need to draw your resist lines on quite quickly or go over the lines lightly with pencil, before they fade.

If you plan to tint the background or paint without resists, you may prefer to draw on to the silk with pencil, because autofade lines will dissolve as soon as they are dampened.

Lilies

Lilies, with their stately beauty and elegance, have inspired artists throughout the ages. There are lots of wonderful varieties, each offering a different delight for the silk painter. My favourites include the lilies with richly-coloured and speckled blooms, and the ones with crisp, curling horns as white as the silk itself.

USING METALLIC OUTLINER

This design is perfect for a cushion cover. It uses gold metallic outliner as a resist. Metallic outliner is easy to apply from a tube, but it does take a little practice. Even tiny gaps in a resist line will allow the dyes to break out. Hold the frame up to the light to check your gutta resist lines. If there are any little gaps or breaks in the lines, repair them before you start painting.

Designs painted with metallic outliner can be washed but not dry-cleaned. The gold metallic outliner remains in the silk after washing. Silk painted with metallic outliner should be ironed on the wrong side.

> **YOU WILL NEED**
> Frame, 45 x 45cm (18 x 18in)
> Three-point silk pins
> Silk crepe de chine
> Dyes: violety blue, violety red, orangey yellow
> Round brushes, Nos. 8 and 10
> Foam brush, 2.5cm (1in)
> Gold metallic outliner
> 3B or charcoal pencil
> Board
> Ruler

The lily design
Enlarge by 385% for a full-size pattern

22

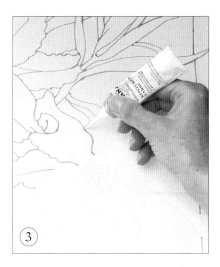

1. Tear or cut the silk to size, along the grain. Pin it on to your frame with the right side (the smoothest side) uppermost. Keep the grain straight and pull the silk taut as you pin so it is stretched evenly and tightly.

2. Place the design under the silk then raise it up slightly using a board until it touches the silk. Trace the design on to the silk very lightly using a pencil. Use a ruler to draw the straight lines for the border. Remove the paper design and board.

3. Outline the design with gold outliner. Make sure that you join up all the lines. When you are sure that there are no gaps in the resist line, leave to dry.

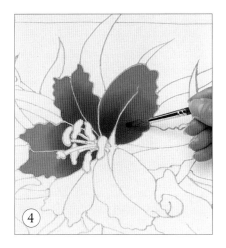

4. Mix your colours then paint the flowers one at a time using a No. 8 brush. Start with orange around the outer edges of the petals, then introduce red. Where the two colours meet, blend them together vigorously with the brush. While the petals are still damp, overpaint with violet towards the centres to shade them.

5. Paint the stamens of each flower purple, and use a light green for the pistils. Leave the stalks of the stamens white.

7. Use a 2.5cm (1in) foam brush to paint the border orange. While the dye is still damp, add an edge of red using a No. 10 brush. Allow the colour to merge into the orange.

6. Paint the centres of the flowers dark green then use blended greens to paint the leaves. Work lighter shades at the tips and deeper tones where the leaves appear under the flowers.

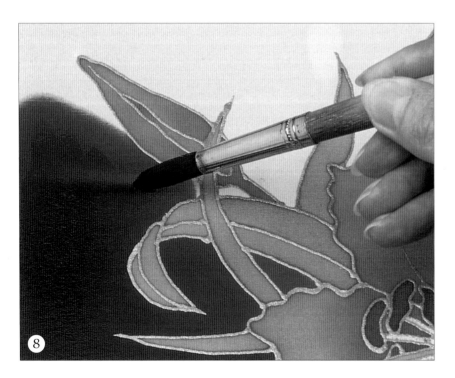

8. Paint the background dark violet. Leave to dry before steam-fixing the colours (see pages 17–18).

The Finished Lily Project

This crepe de chine lily painting has been made up into a cushion cover. It uses gold metallic outliner as a resist and a bold, complementary colour scheme. The petals are painted in blended oranges and reds and over-painted with violet to shade them.

Lily cushions

These sumptuous silk crepe de chine cushions show three different colourways of the lily design featured in this chapter.

Oleanders

I love seeing oleanders in bloom in Mediterranean countries. They are often planted as flowering hedges by the roadside and against walls. They come in all shades of pink, crimson and creamy white. The flowers have a delicious scent and the leaves are dark and spear-shaped.

USING GUTTA RESIST

The most common resist used in silk painting is gutta. Traditional gutta is spirit-based. It is a liquid latex rubber which is totally water-repellent and forms an excellent resist. It can only be removed from the silk by dry-cleaning fluids. For this reason, many silk painters prefer to use the more modern water-based guttas which can be washed out of the silk after fixing.

There is some confusion as to the difference between 'gutta' and 'outliner' and manufacturers do not always agree on terminology. I tend to use the term 'gutta' for a resist which is clear or coloured with dye, and is removed from the silk after fixing, leaving a line which cannot be felt in the silk. I use the term 'outliner' for resists which are heavily pigmented with colour or metallic powders and can still be felt in the silk after washing.

Clear water-based gutta is used for this project. It is applied with a gutta bottle fitted with a gutta nib to achieve fine, even resist lines. Gutta can also be applied from a tube, but I find the nozzle on the tube tends to make a cruder line.

YOU WILL NEED

Frame, 37 x 43cm (14½ x 17in)

Three-point silk pins

Silk crepe de chine

Dyes: violety red, orangey red, orangey yellow, greeny blue, violety blue

Gutta, gutta bottle and nib

Round brushes, Nos. 6 and 8

3B or charcoal pencil or autofade marker

Board

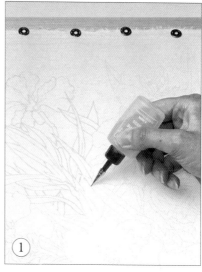

1. Pin up the silk and trace the design very lightly (see page 23) with a pencil or an autofade marker. Remove the paper design and apply the gutta carefully over the traced design. Make sure the gutta penetrates through to the back of the silk and check that there are no gaps or breaks in the resist line. Allow the gutta to dry.

The oleander design

Enlarge by 315% for a full-size pattern

2. Mix your colours, then paint the flowers one at a time using a No. 6 brush. Begin by applying a light pink to the edges of the petals, then work in a mid tone. Finally, add a deep pink to the centre of each flower. Blend the tones into each other (see page 23).

3. Paint the leaves one at a time in tones of green. Begin with a light tone at the tip of the leaf then gradually blend in deeper tones to achieve shading. Paint the stems in a mid-green.

4. Add touches of dark pink to the stems then paint the flower centres yellow.

5. Paint in the background in a very dark bluey grey using a No. 8 brush. Leave to dry. Steam-fix before washing out the gutta with warm water.

Opposite

The Finished Oleander Project

These oleanders are outlined with clear gutta and the colours are carefully blended to create gradations of tone in the flowers and leaves. The dark background gives the painting an oriental look.

Peonies

This painting was inspired by some gorgeous peonies which were growing in my garden. The flowers were drawn straight on to the silk using spirit-based gutta – a good discipline to get you to really observe! Overpainting was used to build up darker edges around the petals and leaves.

Christmas rose

I have a large pot of Christmas roses outside my back door. It is always a delightful surprise to see their strong buds pushing up through the soil in mid winter. Their greeny white flowers are exquisite, each with a complex arrangement of fragile stamens. They withstand gales and snow, and lift the spirits on bleak winter days.

USING CLEAR GUTTA OVER A PAINTED BACKGROUND

The subtle colouration in the line work in this project is achieved by painting the silk with tints of green before outlining the leaves with gutta. This means that when the clear gutta is removed after fixing, some of the linework is white (around the flowers) and the rest is light green. This technique can be used in successive layers of painting so that the lines blend in with the colours used in the design or are 'hidden' (as in the flowers in this project). I have also incorporated the technique of painting on to damp silk (see page 49) in this project.

YOU WILL NEED
Frame, 43 x 43cm (17 x 17in)
Three-point silk pins
Silk habotai
Dyes: orangey yellow, greeny yellow, orangey red, greeny blue, violety blue
Round brushes, Nos. 1, 6, 8 and 10
Mop brush
Gutta, gutta bottle and nib
3B or charcoal pencil
Hairdryer
Board

The Christmas rose design
Enlarge by 375% for a full-size pattern

1. Pin the silk to your frame and trace the design with a pencil. Outline only the flower heads and buds with gutta, making sure that each section is contained. Trace over the stems of the stamens with gutta and apply a line around the outer edge of the border. Allow to dry.

2. Mix your colours, then use neat orange and yellow dye to paint in the stamen heads. Apply the dye in little dots using a No. 1 brush. Dry the dots with a hairdryer as you work to prevent them from spreading. Seal each stamen head with a dot of gutta.

TIP

You can use either spirit- or water-based gutta for this project. If you use spirit-based gutta you can blend straight over the stamens in step 2. Water-based gutta will stain or dissolve if painted over, so you must paint round it carefully.

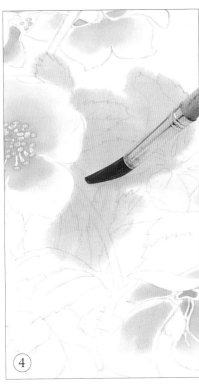

3. Use a No. 8 brush to dampen the flowers and buds with water. Blend a little light yellowy green into the petals, leaving the outer edges and tips white. Introduce a darker tone of green towards the centres of the flowers.

4. Dampen the rest of the silk with water. Use a mop brush for large areas and a No. 6 brush to work carefully around the flowers. Use a No. 10 brush to blend a yellowy green over the leaves and around the border.

5. While the silk is still damp, blend bluey green into some of the leaves and paint an edge of pink around the border. Leave to dry.

6. Outline the leaves, stems and border with gutta. Leave to dry. Overpaint the leaves using a No. 8 brush and shades of green and a little pink. Use the same pink to indicate the stems.

7. Paint the background dark green. Use a No. 10 brush for large areas, and a No. 6 for the spaces between the leaves and flowers.

TIP

To achieve an even background, paint back and forth along the damp spreading edge, overlapping it a little each time. Avoid going back over the wash as it starts to dry.

Opposite

The Finished Christmas Rose Project

The picture in the top right is the finished painting. It is built up in stages, using clear gutta applied over white silk and also over areas which have been painted. In this way the resist lines become less obvious and blend more subtly with the leaves, as shown in the large detail. In some areas, the resist lines are completely concealed.

36

Jasmine

Jasmine scrambles over an old brick wall in my garden and I love to sit beneath it on warm summer nights and breathe in its heady perfume. Clusters of white flowers spring out on the arching stems, spangling the bush with stars and attracting tiny night moths.

USING WAX WITH A BRUSH

Wax is the traditional resist used in batik, and it is a versatile and effective resist when used on silk. It is applied hot, either with a tjanting (see page 42) or with a brush. When brushed on, the wax can be used to mask parts of a painting and so reserve highlights or retain lighter shades of colour. For safety reasons, it is best to melt wax in a thermostatically-controlled wax pot, as it can ignite if overheated.

In this project the jasmine flowers are first painted with wax to retain the white of the silk. A wash of green dye is then applied. The leaves are then waxed, layer by layer over washes of green dye. Each layer of wax masks and retains a shade of green, starting with the lightest shade and finishing with the darkest. This technique is perfect for creating the impression of dense foliage.

It is worth having several different brushes reserved for wax as each brush makes a different sort of mark. Try to avoid brushes which suddenly blob wax as they are infuriating to work with! For this project, I used a small Chinese brush because it had a good point and made the correct shaped marks for the leaves.

YOU WILL NEED

Frame, 43 x 43cm (17 x 17in)
Three-point silk pins
Silk crepe de chine
Dyes: greeny yellow, greeny blue, violety red
Wax and wax pot
Round Chinese brush, No. 7
Foam brush, 2.5cm (1in)
Charcoal pencil
Paper towelling
Plastic gloves
Iron and old newspaper
Gutta, gutta bottle and nib
Board

TIP

If a noticeable residue of wax remains in the silk even after ironing, steam-fix then dry-clean it. Alternatively, steam-fix then rinse it in white spirit. Wash the silk thoroughly in warm, soapy water to remove the white spirit.

The jasmine design

Enlarge by 375% for a full-size pattern

38

1. Trace the design on to silk with a charcoal pencil and draw a line around the edge of the silk with gutta. Leave to dry. Use a Chinese brush to apply wax carefully over the flower petals, leaving the centres of the flowers unwaxed.

TIP

Test the wax on a spare strip of silk before you begin, to make sure it is at the right temperature – it should be transparent when painted on, without white edges. If it foams or bubbles as you touch the brush on the silk, it is too hot.

2. Mix your colours, then use a 2.5cm (1in) foam brush to paint light green all over the silk. Wipe off excess dye with paper towelling (wear plastic gloves when doing this), then leave to dry.

3. Use the Chinese brush to wax in some of the leaves, then repeat step 2 using mid-green. Leave to dry.

TIP

Make sure the painted silk is completely dry before you apply more wax – it will flake off if you try to apply it on damp silk.

4. Wax the rest of the leaves then repeat step 3 using dark green. Again, use paper towelling to wipe excess dye from the waxed areas, then leave to dry.

5. Place about a dozen sheets of old newspaper on your ironing board to protect it. Position the silk on top, then place one sheet of newspaper over that. Iron over the newspaper with a hot, dry iron until the wax melts.

6. Remove the top sheet of newspaper and one from underneath and replace with fresh sheets. Repeat, continuing to strip off the sheets on top and underneath the silk until no more wax irons out. Now move the silk up and do the next section. The silk is now ready to be steam-fixed.

The Finished Jasmine Project

The white jasmine flowers and the dense green foliage in this painting are achieved using successive layers of wax to resist the dye washes. Batik veining can be added to the leaves or flowers (see top right) by unpinning the silk and pinching the wax to crack it, then repinning and applying the dye.

41

Orchids

I find orchids fascinating. I am intrigued by their exotic shapes, strange colours and peculiar markings. They have evolved marvellously complex flower structures, cleverly designed to attract and sometimes trap insects, which ensures pollination.

USING WAX WITH A TJANTING

In this project the resist lines are made with hot wax applied with a tjanting to produce flowing outlines which are worked over a pre-painted background. When the flowers have been painted, the details are added to the petals with a fine brush, using a hairdryer to stop the dye spreading.

The orchid design
Enlarge by 420% for a full-size pattern

YOU WILL NEED

Frame, 49 x 44cm
(19 x 17½in)
Three-point silk pins
Silk habotai
Dyes: violety blue, orangey
red, greeny yellow
Round brushes, Nos. 1 and 6
Foam brush, 2.5cm (1in)
Mop brush
Wax and wax pot
Tjanting
Charcoal pencil
Paper towelling
Iron and old newspaper
Water mister
Gutta, gutta bottle and nib
Hairdryer
Board

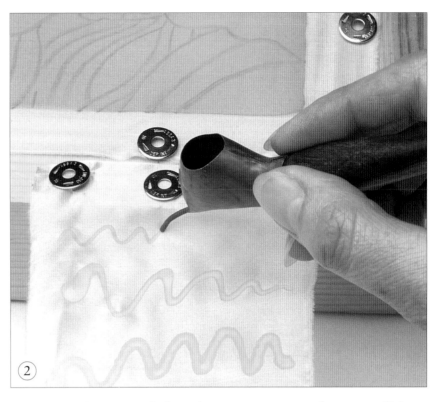

1. Pin the silk on to your frame and draw a line of gutta around the edge of it. Leave to dry. Trace the design with a charcoal pencil. Mix up your colours then use a water mister to dampen the silk. Use a mop brush to blend patches of pale pinks, oranges and greens to cover the silk. Re-tension the silk if necessary. Leave to dry thoroughly.

2. Heat up the wax and place the tjanting into it to heat up. Fill the tjanting then test the temperature of the wax by drawing the spout across a piece of spare silk. The wax should flow freely to form a dark transparent line. If the wax bubbles on the silk or spreads, it is too hot. If it forms a broken or white line it is too cool.

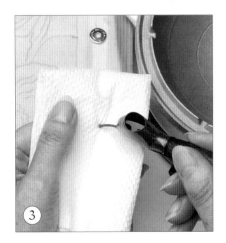

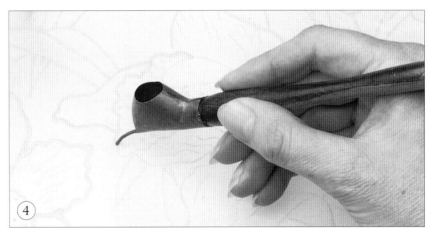

3. Carefully wipe the bowl of the tjanting and block the spout with paper towelling as you move across from the wax pot to the silk – this will prevent the wax from dripping on to your work.

4. Place the spout on the silk and trace over the design lines with wax, but do not outline the patterns in the petals. As soon as the wax ceases to flow freely from the spout, tip it back into the pot and refill it. Check the lines carefully and use the wax to fill in any breaks.

5. Use a No. 6 brush to paint the flowers in various blended shades of pink and green. Introduce darker tones as you work towards the centre of each flower.

7. Paint the leaves and stems in various shades of green. Use dark tones to shade the underside of each leaf.

6. Paint the flower centres, using blended tones of yellow, green and pink.

44

8. Use soft browns to paint in the orchid bulbs. Work green into the centres. Leave the silk to dry thoroughly.

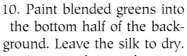

9. Use a No. 1 brush to add tiny dark red spots and lines to the petals. Dab the brush on paper towelling to remove surplus colour as you work, and dry with a hairdryer to prevent the colour from spreading (be careful not to melt the wax as you do this).

10. Paint blended greens into the bottom half of the background. Leave the silk to dry. Iron out the wax between sheets of old newspaper (see page 40) before steam-fixing.

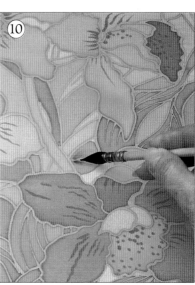

The Finished Orchid Project

These subtly coloured orchids are outlined with a resist of hot wax applied with a tjanting – a traditional Javanese batik tool. I have used muted pinks and greens to convey a steamy tropical atmosphere.

Daffodils

I love to see drifts of wild daffodils growing in dappled sunlight under trees and in long grass, and find few sights as cheering as beds of golden daffodils in parks and gardens in springtime. My seaside garden is rather wind-blown, so I grow the beautiful miniature varieties which withstand rough weather and come up faithfully year after year.

The Finished Daffodil Project
An impression of daffodils in spring sunlight is achieved in this painting by applying the colours directly on to damp silk. The dyes dry with a soft 'out of focus' look.

PAINTING ON DAMP SILK

When you paint on damp silk, the colours seem to spread less than on dry silk because the fibres are already saturated with water and there is nowhere for the dye to go. The painting dries with a soft, blurred 'out of focus' look. You can achieve excellent colour blending on damp silk because the dyes take longer to dry. Usually, more definition can be achieved on heavier silks than on finer ones. Experiment with different silks and try varying the degree of dampness to discover the many exciting effects that can be achieved.

This project is completed in one go before the silk has time to dry. You can use this method as a preliminary stage of a painting, before going on to employ other techniques in it.

The daffodils are freepainted, but I suggest that you place the design underneath the silk and use this as a guide while you paint. Work in a cool room so the silk does not dry too quickly and you do not have to paint too fast! Remember to work darker shades for the flowers in the foreground and lighter tones for the more distant ones.

YOU WILL NEED

Frame, 49 x 43cm (19 x 17in)
Three-point silk pins
Silk crepe georgette
Dyes: greeny yellow, orangey yellow, violety blue, greeny blue, violety red
Round brush, No. 8
Water mister
Gutta, gutta bottle and nib
Polythene
Board

The daffodil design
Enlarge by 870% for a full-size pattern

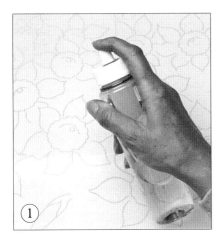

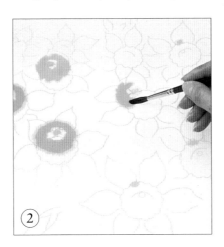

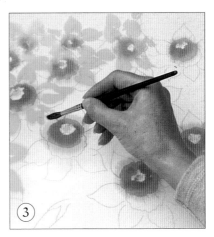

1. Pin the silk on to your frame. Lay a piece of polythene over the design to protect it, then place it underneath, but not touching, the silk. Draw a line of gutta around the edge of the silk. Leave to dry. Spray the silk lightly and evenly with water.

2. Mix your colours. Using the design as a guide, paint the stamens light yellowy green and use orangey yellow for the trumpets.

3. Blend a little orange into each trumpet to give them depth then paint the petals greeny yellow.

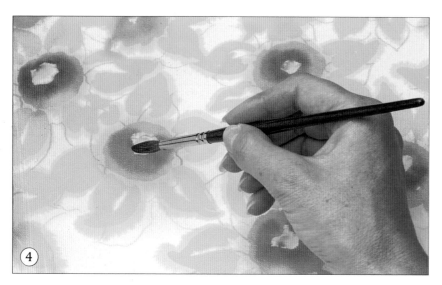

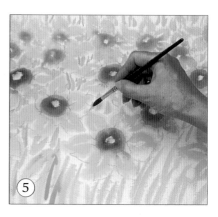

5. Paint the leaves in light and mid greens. Use longer brushstrokes in the foreground and shorter ones in the distance.

4. Blend a little violet into the foreground flower trumpets to add further depth.

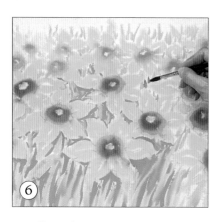

6. Fill in the spaces between the leaves with a darker bluey green. Use the colour sparingly when working the leaves in the distance.

7. Paint the sky using violety blue then use this same sky colour here and there between the flowers and leaves. Blend further violet into the flower heads in the foreground to add shade. Leave to dry then steam-fix.

TIP

Leave crepe georgette and chiffon to dry naturally – do not dry with a hairdryer as this spoils the dye surface and makes watermarks. Other silks can be gently dried with a hairdryer when the colours have merged as much as you want them to.

Opposite
Daffodil scarf
This long silk georgette daffodil scarf uses the same method of painting on damp silk as shown in the project.

Mallows

Annual mallows seed themselves and grow into bushy hedges covered in glossy pink flowers each summer. I photographed some mallows a while ago, and painted this textile design using the photographs for reference. I wanted to capture the delicacy of the sugar-pink blooms and the contrast of this colour against the lush garden foliage.

PAINTING ON DRY SILK

This project is painted directly on to silk without preliminary drawing. Mallows are a simple shape so they are ideal for the technique of painting without resists (more complex shapes can be more difficult to achieve due to the nature of the spreading dyes). The flowers are painted first, using a little colour blending on damp silk, and they are then dried. The foliage is added in small dabs of overlapping greens. Remember that dye spreads very freely on dry silk and in this project there are no resist lines to contain the spread – therefore, do not apply the green too generously or your flowers will be engulfed by the colour! The greens should spread only slightly across each other and across the edges of the pink flowers, to create ragged edges.

There is no pattern for this project, but you should draw in the flowers very roughly using an autofade marker. The autofade marker lines act as a temporary guide to the positioning of the flowers and they will dissolve away as soon as you paint over them.

The veins of the leaves and petals are worked using light, quick strokes and a fairly dry brush. It is a good idea to practise on a spare piece of silk before you start.

YOU WILL NEED
Frame, 36 x 42cm (14 x 16½in)
Three-point silk pins
Silk habotai
Dyes: violety red, violety blue, greeny yellow
Round brush, No. 8
Rigger brush, No. 4
Hairdryer
Gutta, gutta bottle and nib
Paper towelling
Autofade marker

Opposite

The Finished Mallow Project

These shiny pink mallow blooms are painted directly on to dry silk habotai. It takes a little practice to judge how far the dyes will spread – a hairdryer becomes a useful friend for stopping the colours in mid flow!

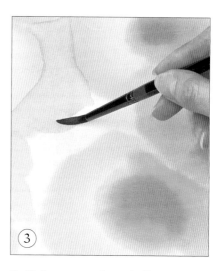

1. Pin the silk on to your frame then draw a line of gutta around the edge of it. Leave to dry. Use an autofade marker to roughly sketch the position of the flowers. Mix your colours, then use a No. 8 brush to paint water into one of the circles. Outline the circle with light pink. Repeat, painting in each flower one at a time.

2. While the dye is still damp, paint deep pink into the centre of each flower. Soften the edges on one side of each bloom, making sure that you retain a white area of silk – this will make the flowers look glossy. Dry evenly with a hairdryer.

3. Paint around each flower using the lightest green. Allow the colour to shape the wavy edge of the petals. Dry with a hairdryer.

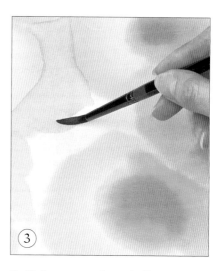

4. Paint in the leaves using mid greens. Dry with a hairdyer as you work. Introduce some dark green to add depth to the foliage and to define the leaves further. Again, dry with a hairdryer.

5. Use a No. 4 rigger brush and dark green to paint veins along some of the leaves.

54

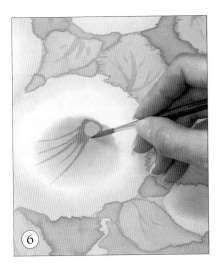

6. Use the same method as in the previous step to paint violety red veins on the flower petals. Carefully work in a dark red shadow in the centre of each flower. Leave the stamens unpainted. As you work, use the hairdryer to stop the colours spreading. When dry, steam fix.

TIP

When painting veins, dab excess dye on to paper towelling before you touch the brush on the silk. This will avoid too much colour flooding in.

Dandelion, petunia and hibiscus scarves

These floral scarves are painted on dry crepe georgette. A little clear gutta is used to give definition to the centres. When working on transparent silks like crepe georgette and chiffon, do not use a hairdryer – let the dyes soak in and dry naturally.

Tulips

I had an old friend who kept a beautiful cottage garden next to my studio. He was a traditional, old-fashioned gardener who grew vegetables and flowers alongside each other. Every season his flower beds held new delights. One spring he had beautiful cream tulips growing amongst rich red and gold wallflowers. The bed was edged with forget-me-nots and deep blue hyacinths. In the mornings, the sun filled the tulips with light, making them float like moons above a sea of colour. The beautiful combination of colours and textures was the inspiration for this project, and I worked from a coloured pencil sketch I made at the time.

PAINTING WITH BROKEN COLOUR

This project uses the technique of applying little dabs of colour on to dry silk to create the effect of a mass of flowers around the tulips. The tulips are painted first, then sealed with wax to define them and to stop the other colours spreading into them. It can be difficult to apply gutta on heavy silks such as crepe de chine so that it forms an effective resist, so wax is a better choice for this silk. Before you begin, you will need to heat up the wax in a wax pot.

The broken colour technique is also very effective for paintings on silk velvet and other heavier silks. It produces an effect similar to that of pointillism – a technique developed by Seurat in the 1880s, which used dots of colour which, when viewed from a distance, would mingle and harmonise to give the effect of sparkling light.

Opposite

Orange tulips

These bold orange tulips are a variation of the project piece shown on pages 60–61. They are painted on to dry crepe de chine without the use of wax. The result is free, informal-looking flowers with ragged edges. The background is textured with small dabs of broken colour in complementary tints.

YOU WILL NEED

Frame, 50 x 42cm (19½ x 16½in)

Three-point silk pins

Silk crepe de chine

Dyes: orangey red, greeny yellow, orangey yellow, violety blue

Round brush, No. 8

Wax brush, No. 8 (with a good point)

Wax and wax pot

Charcoal pencil

Water mister

Gutta, gutta bottle and nib

Paper towelling

Hairdryer

Iron and old newspaper

Board

The tulip design
Enlarge by 425% for a full-size pattern

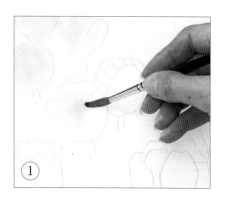

1. Pin the silk on to your frame. Draw a line of gutta around the edge and leave to dry. Trace the design on to the silk very lightly using a charcoal pencil. Mix your colours, then spray the silk evenly with water. Freely paint over the tulip heads with light yellow using a No. 8 brush. The colour will spread slightly beyond the lines at this stage.

2. While the silk is still damp, use a deeper yellow to shade around the edge and into the centre of each flower. Dry with a hairdryer.

58

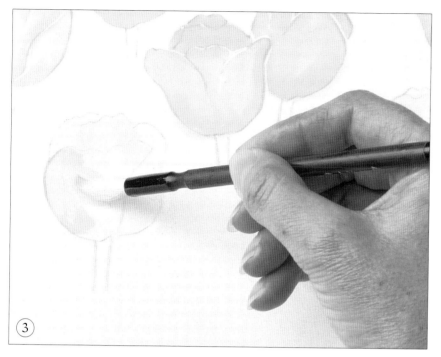

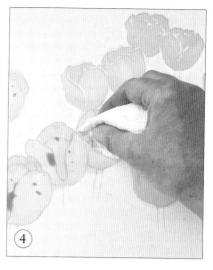

3. Wax over each flower head using a No. 8 wax brush. Leave spaces between the petals, using the design lines as a guide. Do not wax over the stems.

4. Brush over the flower heads with the darker yellow to fill in the gaps between the petals. Wipe off any surplus dye from the wax with paper towelling before it dries. Do not worry if a little dye seeps into the surrounding silk.

5. Paint over the stems with a light green. Add a little darker green under the flower head while the silk is still damp. You can dry the stems gently with a hairdryer as you work, to stop the green spreading too far, but be careful not to melt the wax. Leave to dry then wax over the stems and over the gaps between the petals to seal them.

6. Paint in the mass of wallflowers and forget-me-nots in little dabs of colour. Dry gently with a hairdryer as you work, to stop the dots spreading into each other. Build up the colours and tones, adding darker colours to increase the sense of depth in the foliage. Iron out the wax between sheets of newspaper (see page 40), then steam-fix.

The Finished Tulip Project

Wax is used to mask and define the pale yellow tulips in this painting. The mass of wallflowers and forget-me-nots are painted freely on to dry silk with small brushstrokes of colour.

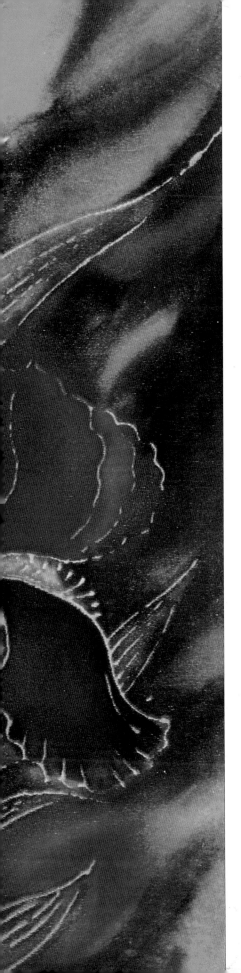

Irises

Painters have always loved irises, especially the large bearded varieties which grow in spreading clumps. They have dramatic fans of broad leaves, and tall stems which bear silky, fabulously-patterned flowers. They can be seen in a range of amazing colours – from delicate pinks, blues and lilacs to warm apricots, yellows and strangely speckled bronzes. I love the rich velvety purple ones with 'beards' like bright yellow, fluffy caterpillars.

The Finished Iris Project

You can achieve stunning effects on silk velvet. The pile produces very rich colours which shimmer in the light. In this painting of purple bearded irises, the outlines have been etched to give the flowers some definition and to reduce colour spread.

ETCHING ON SILK VELVET

This project is worked on silk/viscose velvet as the fabric is so reminiscent of the texture of the irises. Resists are not very effective on velvet due to the thickness of the pile, so the linear design has been etched out of the velvet pile using a special paste which can be purchased from silk painting suppliers and some craft shops. It works well on silk/viscose velvet, as it burns out the cellulose viscose pile, leaving the silk backing intact.

In this project, the outlines of the irises and some of the leaves are etched out. The etched lines give the painting some linear definition and a slightly 'quilted' appearance. They also help to stop the dyes spreading into adjoining areas during painting. The lines only act as a partial barrier however, so some colour blending does occur, which tends to enhance the quality of the painting.

Read through the project carefully before you begin and practise applying the gel on a spare piece of velvet and then ironing it. Do not set the iron too hot and do not iron for too long or you will turn the lines of etching gel black and burn holes in the velvet.

WARNING

Etching gel must be used with care and in a well-ventilated area. Always follow the manufacturer's instructions carefully and wear plastic gloves when working with it.

YOU WILL NEED

Frame, 47 x 50cm (18½ x 19½in)

Stenter pins

Silk/viscose velvet

Dyes: violety blue, violety red, orangey yellow, greeny yellow, greeny blue

Etching gel

Round brush, No. 12

Autofade marker

Plastic gloves

Iron

Hairdryer

Board

The iris design

Enlarge by 370% for a full-size pattern

1

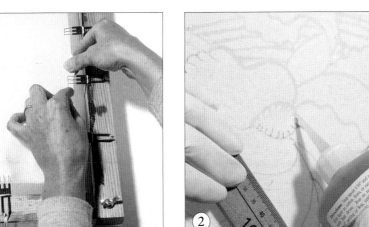

2

TIP

You may find it easier to apply a steady line of etching gel if you support your wrist on a yardstick or a piece of flat wood laid across the frame. Start in the top left-hand corner (if you are right-handed) and work your way down. This will prevent you from smudging the lines.

1. Loop stenter pins around the frame and through the elastic bands. Ensure that the velvet is pile side down, then hook the pins on to the edge of the fabric.

2. Trace the design using an autofade marker. Remove the design and board. Outline the design with etching gel, applied in the same way as you would gutta. Dry the gel with a hairdryer.

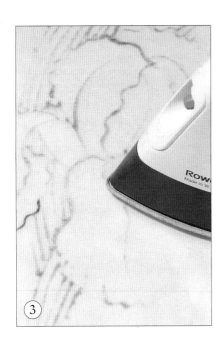

3

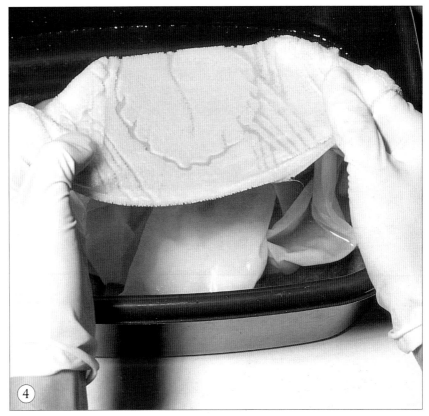

4

3. Remove the silk from the frame. Place it pile side down on your ironing board and carefully iron it using a dry iron on the silk/wool setting. Continue ironing until the lines change to a light brown colour and become brittle.

4. Rinse the velvet gently in water until the pile in the linear design drops away. Allow to dry.

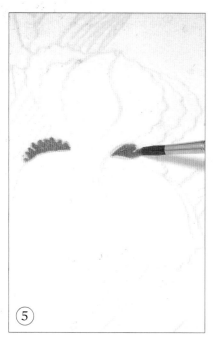

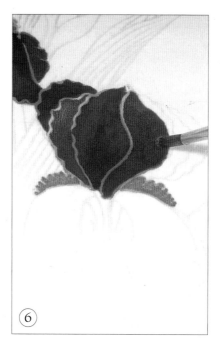

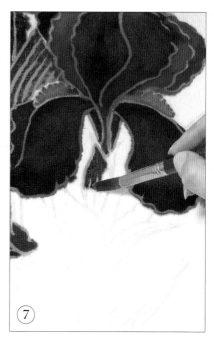

5. Pin the silk back on to your frame, pile side up. Mix your colours, then paint the flower stamens yellow using a No. 12 brush. Dry with a hairdryer to stop the dye spreading.

6. Paint the iris petals in blended violets and blues, leaving a margin around the stamens to allow for the spread of the dyes. Dry the area around the stamens to stop the colours spreading across into the yellow.

7. Paint the leaves and stems using bright and dull greens.

8. Paint violet into areas of the background to suggest distant buds and petals, and work dark tones between and around some of the leaves to create depth. Blend bright and dull greens into the rest of the background. Leave the velvet to dry thoroughly. Unpin the velvet, then steam-fix using two layers of cloth or steaming paper to absorb surplus dye. Rinse in cold running water, short spin then line- or tumble-dry for a short time.

TIP

Velvet can be ironed while still slightly damp to increase the sheen. Use the iron on a silk setting and press the pile in the direction of the nap (as if you were stoking a cat!).

Purple and gold irises
Wonderfully sumptuous effects can be achieved on velvet using the etching technique and a rich palette of colours. It is important to always mix and blend your colours well when working on silk velvet.

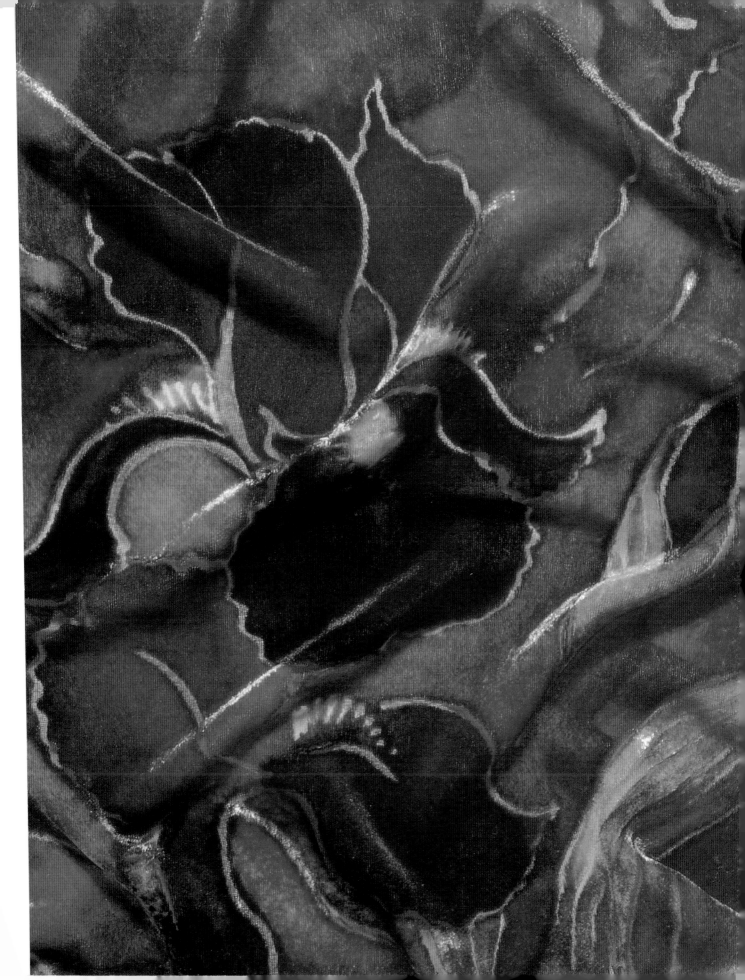

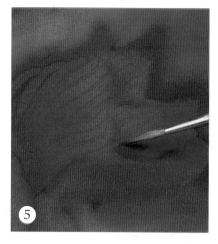

4. Paint the background using blended blues and violets. Use lighter tones of blue in the central areas between the flowers. Leave to dry naturally.

5. Use a No. 4 rigger brush to add streaks of diffusing medium to the petals to create veins. Control the spread of the diffusing medium by drying with a hairdryer when you are happy with the effect.

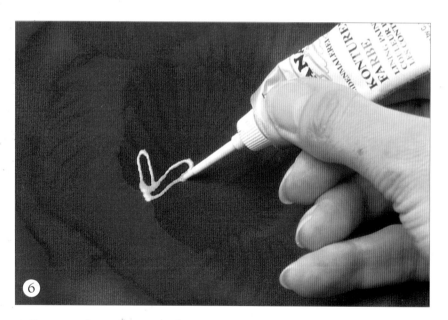

6. Draw in the stamens with metallic gold outliner. Leave to dry before steam-fixing.

The Finished Amaryllis Project

These rich red amaryllis blooms are on silk georgette. The petal veins are created by painting over the dry red dye with brushstrokes of diffusing medium. The diffusing medium drives back the dye to create light lines with dark edges. Metallic gold outliner is added as an ornate touch for the stamens when the rest of the painting is finished.

Hibiscus

I have a beautiful blue hibiscus in my garden which bursts into bloom in mid summer. The flowers are a marvellous shade of clear violet blue, flushed with crimson in the centres, and the stamens form little cream-coloured cones which extend from the flower centres. In certain lights, the blue flowers seem to glow against the bright green foliage.

The Finished Hibiscus Project

These stunning blue hibiscus flowers are painted on silk habotai treated with anti-spread medium. This controls the spread of the dyes and makes it more like painting on paper!

72

USING ANTI-SPREAD

In traditional Chinese painting and early European silk painting, the silk was treated with natural gums and starches so that the colours would not spread. This method can be used in modern silk painting to achieve effects similar to watercolour painting on paper, but with the advantage of being able to use the strong, pure colours that you get with dyes. Different ranges of silk dyes and paints are supplied with their own anti-spread medium. Alternatively, you can mix your own by adding water to thickener.

In this project the whole piece of silk is treated. You can, however, just treat certain areas of a painting, so that fine details such as veins in petals or leaves may be painted. Anti-spread can be painted over pre-painted areas too, although some dye disturbance will occur if the dyes have not been fixed. Anti-spread is washed out of the silk with warm water after steaming.

> ## YOU WILL NEED
> **Frame, 44 x 44cm (17 x 17in)**
> **Three-point silk pins**
> **Silk habotai**
> **Dyes: violety blue, violety red, greeny yellow**
> **Round brush, No. 8 (with a good point)**
> **Foam brush, 2.5cm (1in)**
> **Anti-spread**
> **Charcoal pencil**

1. Pin the silk on to your frame. Trace the design very lightly with a charcoal pencil. Pour the anti-spread medium into a palette then paint it on to the silk evenly using a foam brush. Adjust the pins to re-tension the silk. Leave to dry.

The hibiscus design

Enlarge by 330% for a full-size pattern

2. Mix your colours, then use a No. 8 brush to paint the flowers one by one in blended tones of blue. Work carefully around the central stamens to leave them white. While the dye is still wet, blend pink into the base of the petals. Leave to dry.

3. Paint in the stamens using dots of creamy yellow, applied with the tip of the brush.

4. Add veining to the petals using undiluted dark red and the tip of the brush.

5. Paint in the leaves using various shades of green, starting with the lightest. Use a dark bluey green in the background to add depth to the foliage. Dry the silk then steam-fix it. Rinse the anti-spread out in lukewarm water to restore the soft handle of the silk.

Opposite
Poppies
Poppies, with their delicious colours and silky petals, are favourite subjects to paint on silk. This bed of poppies is painted on silk crepe de chine treated with anti-spread medium.

74

Poppies

A field of poppies is a wonderful sight but sadly one not often seen now, due to the use of pesticides and weed killers. However, even a verge of scarlet poppies beside a road turns heads and brings a moment of pleasure to passing motorists.

DISCHARGING WITH ILLUMINANTS

Discharging using illuminants is a method of bleaching out colour from a dyed fabric and replacing it with another colour. It is a way of achieving light or bright colours on a dark background. A reducing agent (discharge salt) is used to remove areas of colour. Illuminants (dyes which are unaffected by the reducing agent) are mixed with the discharge salt so that as one colour is bleached out, a new one takes its place. Water can be mixed with the illuminant to make a lighter colour.

Discharging materials are available from specialist silk painting suppliers. Also, experiment with your own dyes to discover which will discharge successfully. Remember to wear plastic gloves, and follow the manufacturer's instructions carefully.

YOU WILL NEED

Frame, 50 x 34cm (19½ x 13½in)

Stenter pins

Silk/viscose velvet

Round brushes, Nos 8 and 12

Dischargeable silk painting dyes: greeny blue, violety blue, greeny yellow

Illuminant: orangey red

Plastic gloves

Thickener

Discharge salt

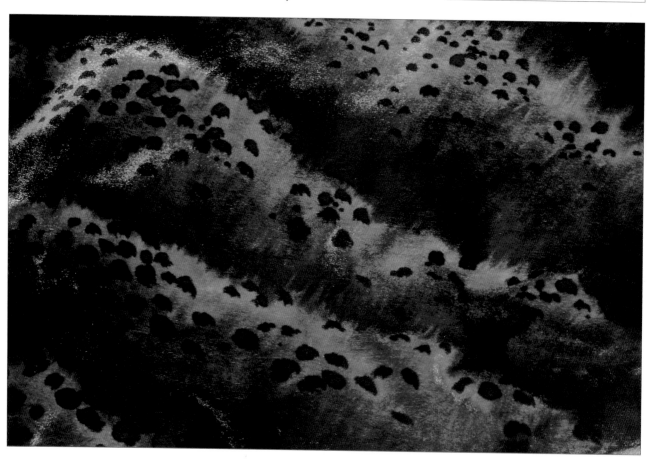

1. Wear plastic gloves to mix ¼tsp of discharge salt with 10ml of thickener. Stir until the salt has dissolved. Mix in 10ml of red illuminant. Test on a spare piece of silk to check the strength of the colour and the consistency of the paste – it should paint on easily and it should not spread.

2. Pin the silk, pile side up, on to the frame using stenter pins. Mix your colours, then paint the grassy background using a No. 12 brush. Begin with bands of light greens, worked in bold diagonal brushstrokes to suggest blades of grass.

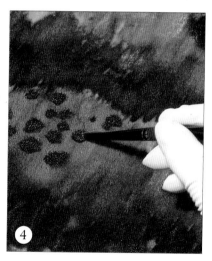

3. Introduce darker greens to create the effect of patches of shadow in a grassy field. Leave to dry.

Opposite

The Finished Poppy Project

This painting on silk velvet features bright red poppies sharply defined against green grass. The poppies are added using discharging salt and a red illuminant, which means there is no need for a linear division of resist between the two colours.

4. Paint the poppies using a No. 8 brush and the red paste. The red looks dark on the silk at this stage. Leave to dry, then steam the silk in the usual way, using one or two extra layers of paper or cloth to absorb the surplus dye in the thickener.

Wild roses

Roses have been favourite subjects for painters and designers for centuries. There are wonderful old and new varieties of cultivated roses in many different colours and formations, but I always think there is something especially pleasing about the simple, delicate wild roses which grow in tangled profusion in the hedgerows in summer.

USING SALT

This project uses salt to create texture in the leaves. It is sprinkled on to the painted silk while the dye is still damp and patterns appear after a few minutes, as if by magic, and continue to increase until the silk is dry. The effect can be stopped at any time by gently drying with a hairdryer. Do not heap the salt on, as it will take out too much colour and spoil the patterning – use just a fine sprinkling. Flick off any grains from resist lines as they will filter the colour across and cause 'bleeds' into adjacent sections.

Lots of different types of salt can be used for this technique – fine cooking salt makes delicate texturing for small flowers or foliage, and coarse rock or sea salt produces bolder patterns which are ideal for larger leaves or backgrounds. An even-grain 'effect salt' is sold by silk painting suppliers.

YOU WILL NEED

Frame, 29 x 29cm (11½ x 11½in)

Three-point silk pins

Silk habotai

Dyes: greeny blue, violety blue, violety red, orangey yellow

Round brush, No. 8

Fine salt

Charcoal pencil or autofade marker

Gutta, gutta bottle and nib

Hairdryer

Board

1. Pin up the silk. Trace the design and outline with gutta. Leave to dry. Paint the flowers and background. Leave to dry. Paint in the green leaves, working small areas at a time. While they are still damp, sprinkle on fine salt.

2. Leave for approximately one minute then dry the silk gently with a hairdryer. Brush off the salt with your hand to reveal the patterning. Ensure that all grains have been removed before steam-fixing the colours.

The wild rose design
Enlarge by 520% for a full-size pattern

The Finished Wild Rose Design
I used the design above as the basis for a much larger piece – a section of which is shown here. Fine cooking salt was used to mottle the leaves.

Index

My Place

Published by Collins Dove
A Division of HarperCollins*Publishers* (Australia) Pty Ltd
22–24 Joseph Street
North Blackburn, Victoria 3130.

Illustrated and designed by Donna Rawlins
Typeset in Century by Propaganda Typesetting, Glebe
Colour separations by ColourScan Overseas Pty Ltd
Produced in Hong Kong

First published 1988
Reprinted 1988 (three times), 1989, 1990, 1991, 1992, 1993

National Library of Australia
Cataloguing-in-Publication data:
Wheatley, Nadia, 1949.
  My Place.
  ISBN 0 85924 609 4
  1. Australia—History—Juvenile fiction. I. Rawlins, Donna, 1956– . II. Title.
A823'8

My Place

Nadia Wheatley and Donna Rawlins

CollinsDove
A Division of HarperCollinsPublishers

1988

My name's Laura and this is my place. I turned ten last week. Our house is the one with the flag on the window. Tony says it shows we're on Aboriginal land, but I think it means the colour of the earth, back home. Mum and Dad live here too, and Terry and Lorraine, and Auntie Bev, and Tony and Diane and their baby Dean. He's my nephew and he's so cute! We come from Bourke, but Dad thought there'd be more jobs in the city.

This is me and Gully. I have to keep her on a lead because she chases cars. She comes from Bourke too. I guess she thinks they're sheep.

This is a map of my place. We've got a McDonalds right on the corner! In the McDonalds yard, there's this big tree, and whenever I sit in it, it always makes me feel good. There's a canal down the bottom of the street, and Mum says it must have been a creek once. It's too dirty to swim in, but Tony made me a tin canoe and now some of the other kids are making them too. If you tip over and go in, the water tastes yucky and your parents go wild.

For my birthday, Mum said we could have tea at McDonalds! We sat in the outside bit, under the tree, and it felt just like home.

Church and graveyard
My new School
Cop shop
Cakes Pies
old furniture
Lebanese takeaway
Post Office
newspapers
Service station
Old Junk yard
THE BICENTENNIAL HOTEL
St Vde P OP SHOP
Vietnamese cafe
Greek deli
Bread shop
Park view restaurant
Thai restaurant
empty
Hamburgers
Dry-cleaner
RAILWAY PUB
STATION
chimneys

THEY'RE BULL DOZING IN THE OLD TIP
FLATS
FLATS
FLATS
houses
BIG TREE WITH LAWN UNDER IT
McDONALDS
CAR PARK
LANE
Vietnamese Grocery
TRAFFIC LIGHTS
FLATS
FLATS
My friend Tamara lives here
TRUCK YARD
houses
My friend Fatima lives here
LANE
warehouse
CANAL

My friend Bianca lives here
All this colour is houses
MY PLACE → HOME
My friend Soriya lives here
LANE

This road is really busy. Gully isn't allowed up here.
There's a bridge over that way along the canal but I couldn't fit it in. Planes fly that way.

BRICK PITS PARK
It's only just opened this year

chimneys

TRACK (THERE'S A FENCE WITH LOTS OF GOOD HOLES)

OLD FACTORIES AND STUFF
OLD WOODEN BUILDINGS

1978

This is my place. I'm Mike. I'm nearly seven. I live with Mum and Dad and Yaya and Auntie Sofia. Yaya's my grandmother, but I call her that because she's Greek. I don't speak very much Greek, but I kind of always understand what she's saying.

We have Easter lunch in the backyard under the grapevine. There's roast lamb and salad, and of course I get chocolate eggs, but we have red real eggs too, and we have a competition about cracking them. I'm the best at it.

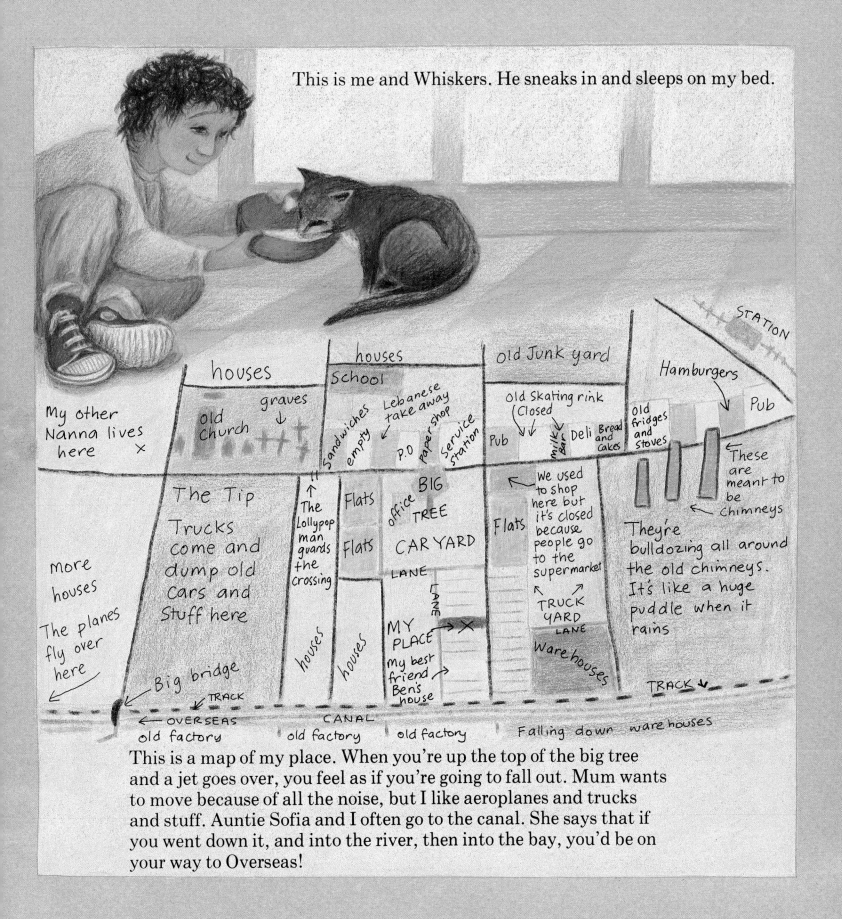

This is me and Whiskers. He sneaks in and sleeps on my bed.

This is a map of my place. When you're up the top of the big tree and a jet goes over, you feel as if you're going to fall out. Mum wants to move because of all the noise, but I like aeroplanes and trucks and stuff. Auntie Sofia and I often go to the canal. She says that if you went down it, and into the river, then into the bay, you'd be on your way to Overseas!

1968

My name's Sofia and this is my place. I'm ten. Baba's just painted our house blue. He comes from Greece, and he says lots of houses on his island were this colour. I think it's really pretty. I live with Mama and Baba and Maroula and Paul McCartney. I've got a big brother called Michaelis, but he's a soldier in Vietnam. Mama lights candles to pray that he comes home soon and isn't hurt.

This is me and Paul McCartney. Maroula reckons John Lennon's best, but I like Paul.

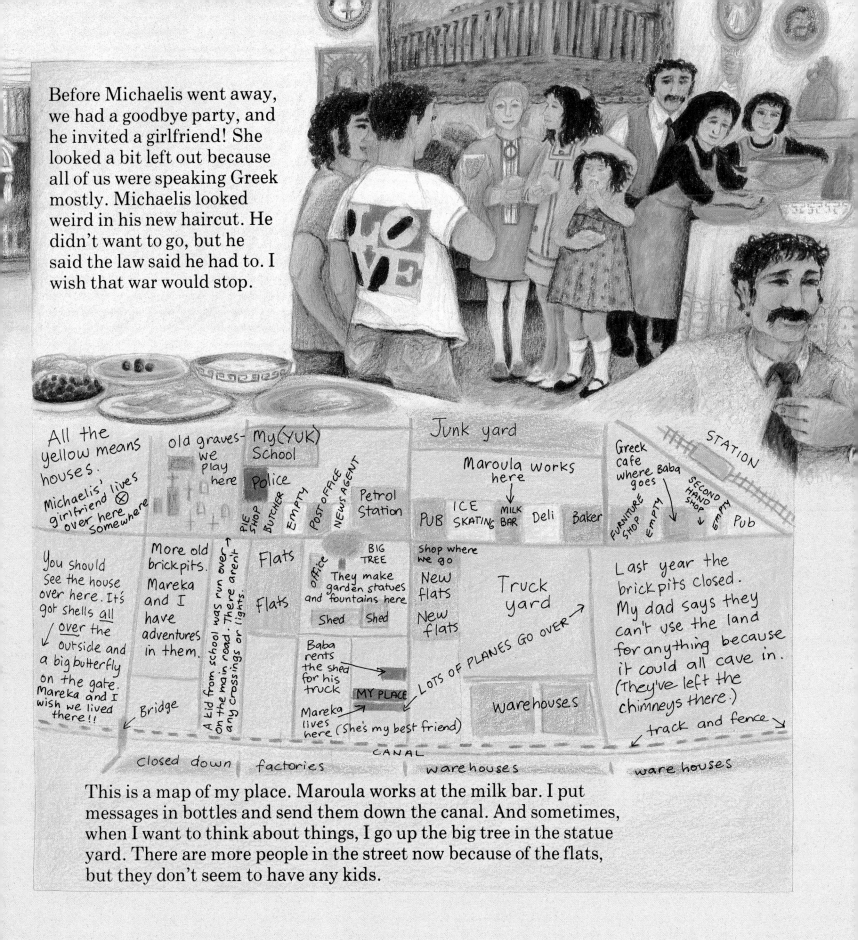

Before Michaelis went away, we had a goodbye party, and he invited a girlfriend! She looked a bit left out because all of us were speaking Greek mostly. Michaelis looked weird in his new haircut. He didn't want to go, but he said the law said he had to. I wish that war would stop.

All the yellow means houses.

Michaelis' girlfriend lives over here Somewhere ⊗

old graves- we play here

My (YUK) School

Police

PIE SHOP BUTCHER EMPTY POST OFFICE NEWS AGENT

Petrol Station

Junk yard

Maroula works here

ICE SKATING MILK BAR Deli Baker

PUB

Greek cafe where Baba goes

STATION

FURNITURE SHOP EMPTY SECOND HAND SHOP EMPTY Pub

You should see the house over here. It's got shells all over the outside and a big butterfly on the gate. Mareka and I wish we lived there!!

More old brickpits. Mareka and I have adventures in them.

Bridge

A kid from school was run over on the main road. There aren't any crossings or lights.

Flats

Flats

office

BIG TREE

They make garden statues and fountains here

Shed Shed

Baba rents the shed for his truck

MY PLACE

Mareka lives here (She's my best friend)

Shop where we go

New flats

New flats

Truck yard

LOTS OF PLANES GO OVER →

Warehouses

Last year the brickpits closed. My dad says they can't use the land for anything because it could all cave in. (They've left the chimneys there.)

track and fence ↘

CANAL

Closed down factories

warehouses

ware houses

This is a map of my place. Maroula works at the milk bar. I put messages in bottles and send them down the canal. And sometimes, when I want to think about things, I go up the big tree in the statue yard. There are more people in the street now because of the flats, but they don't seem to have any kids.

1958

This is my place. My name's Michaelis but at school I say it's Mick. I'm eleven. I was born on Kalymnos but my parents moved here because there wasn't enough work on our island. Baba used to be a sponge diver but now he drives a taxi. Mama sews shirts at home, so she doesn't learn to speak English much. I've already got a sister called Maroula, and now I've got a new one called Sofia. You'd think at least one of them could have been a boy.

After Sofia got christened, we had a party. Baba and I had to make a fence so no one would tread on the new grape vine. Sometimes I think there are more Greek people around here than there are on Kalymnos.

This is a map of my place. Pop and Mrs Malcolm next door have got a television, and sometimes they let me go in and watch it! Up near the depot there's a big tree, and I play Tarzan. That and Zorro are my favourite shows. Sometimes at the end of the day our family goes for a little walk beside the canal, like we used to do around the harbour back on Kalymnos. It's pretty dirty, and there aren't any cafes or anything, but Mama says if you shut your eyes you can pretend it's the Aegean.

That stupid girl that kissed me lives over here ✗

houses

Church but not ours

old grave.

I go to school here

More old brickpits

Taxi rank where Baba often works from ✗

STATION

Police

Pies

Butcher

fruit shop

P.O

Paper shop

The new service station

It's closing soon

You can buy Greek bread here

BIG Pub

PICTURE THEATRE

MILK BAR

Deli

Baker

Pub Closed

Railway Pub

MAIN ROAD—LOTS OF TRUCKS AND MOTOR BIKES!!

houses

The old brickpits here are closed. Mama says they're dangerous but we play in them

my mate Christos lives here

Flats

Flats

BIG TREE

OFFICE

TRUCK DEPOT

TRUCKS PARK HERE

DELI

my friend Nick's dad has this deli.

They're knocking down the old soft drink factory ✗

BRICK PITS ✗ ✗

They still use these ones, but not much

X's mean chimneys

My friends and I ride our bikes along the track.

HOUSES

HOUSES

Lane

HOUSES old shed

HOUSES

MY PLACE

Lane

My friend Wayne lives here →

My friend Manolis lives here ↑

warehouses

There's a fence along the canal but it has good holes

track

Pop and Mrs malcolm's place →

Bridge →

Shirt factory that Mama works for

CANAL ↑

WE GO FOR WALKS ALONG HERE

These two factories are closed down

Bed spring factory

warehouse

warehouse

warehouse

warehouse

warehouse

warehouse →

This is me and my silkworms. They don't have names. I feed them on mulberry leaves. Their silk is soft and golden.

1948

My name's Jen and this is my place. I'm eight and a half. I live with Mum and Grandpa and Auntie Bridie, and now there's my new dad. My real dad's dead. He went to the war before I was born, so I never even saw him. But Mum says I've got his hair.

When Mum married my new dad, we had a party. Uncle Paddy and Uncle Col came, and Miss Miller from next door and the Malcolms from the other side. Miss Miller's going to be ninety next year! My new dad's got a car. It's green.

This is a map of my place. Mum says when she was a kid there used to be heaps more shops. They're knocking the Haunted House down, but Miss Miller yelled at them and made them promise not to touch the big tree. She told them I've got a swing in it. At the bottom of the street there's a canal. The Council's built a fence, but it always seems to get holes in it. Sometimes I fish down there, but I never catch anything.

This is me and Soxie. Dad says we might move out to the western suburbs soon, and get a house with a big yard all around it. But I think Soxie would hate it. He likes how it smells here.

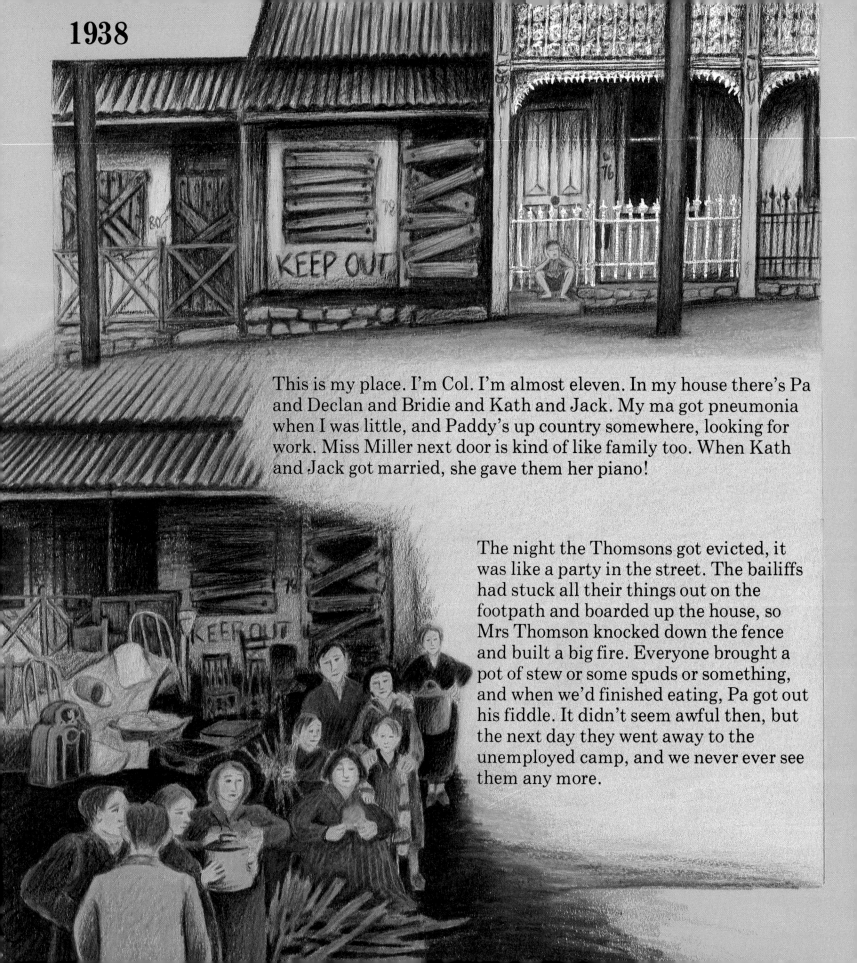

1938

This is my place. I'm Col. I'm almost eleven. In my house there's Pa and Declan and Bridie and Kath and Jack. My ma got pneumonia when I was little, and Paddy's up country somewhere, looking for work. Miss Miller next door is kind of like family too. When Kath and Jack got married, she gave them her piano!

The night the Thomsons got evicted, it was like a party in the street. The bailiffs had stuck all their things out on the footpath and boarded up the house, so Mrs Thomson knocked down the fence and built a big fire. Everyone brought a pot of stew or some spuds or something, and when we'd finished eating, Pa got out his fiddle. It didn't seem awful then, but the next day they went away to the unemployed camp, and we never ever see them any more.

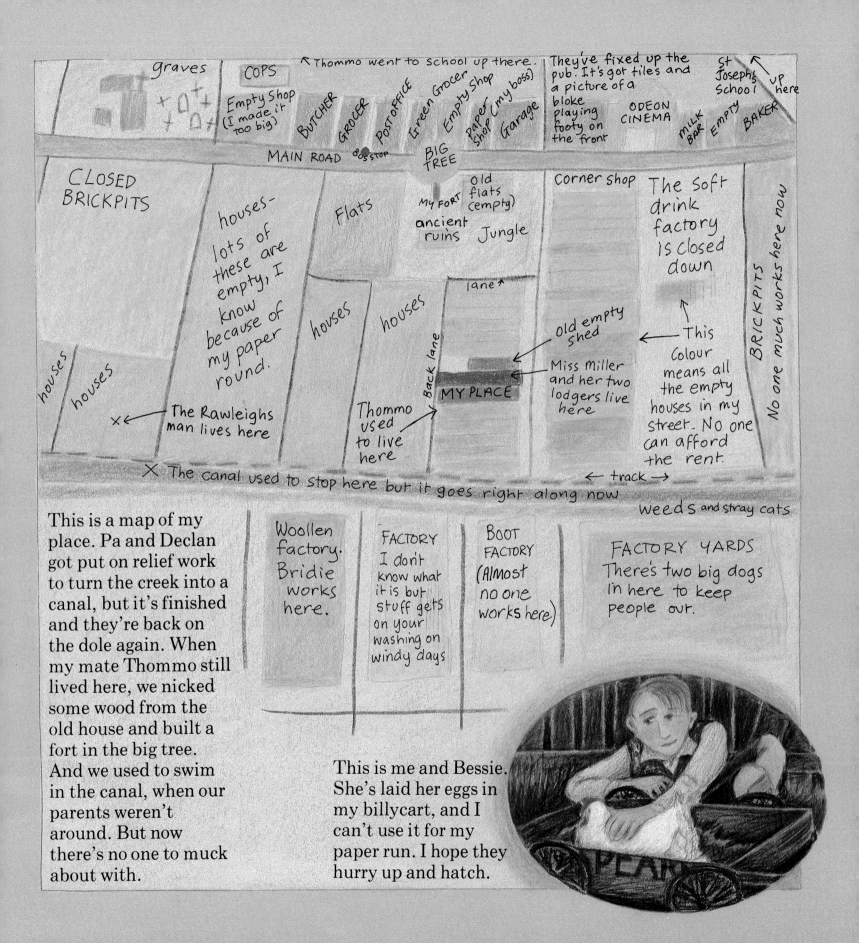

graves

COPS

↑ Thommo went to school up there.

Empty Shop (I made it too big)

BUTCHER

GROCER

POST OFFICE

Green Grocer

Empty Shop

Paper Shop (my boss)

Garage

They've fixed up the pub. It's got tiles and a picture of a bloke playing footy on the front

ODEON CINEMA

St Joseph's School ↑ up here

MILK BAR

EMPTY

BAKER

MAIN ROAD   BUS STOP   BIG TREE

CLOSED BRICKPITS

houses— lots of these are empty, I know because of my paper round.

Flats

MY FORT

ancient ruins

Old flats (empty)

Jungle

Corner shop

The Soft drink factory is closed down

No one much works here now

houses

houses

houses

houses

× ← The Rawleighs man lives here

Thommo used to live here

Back lane

lane ↗

MY PLACE

Old empty shed

Miss miller and her two lodgers live here

← This colour means all the empty houses in my street. No one can afford the rent.

BRICKPITS

× The canal used to stop here but it goes right along now

← track →

weeds and stray cats

This is a map of my place. Pa and Declan got put on relief work to turn the creek into a canal, but it's finished and they're back on the dole again. When my mate Thommo still lived here, we nicked some wood from the old house and built a fort in the big tree. And we used to swim in the canal, when our parents weren't around. But now there's no one to muck about with.

Woollen factory. Bridie works here.

FACTORY I don't know what it is but stuff gets on your washing on windy days

BOOT FACTORY (Almost no one works here)

FACTORY YARDS There's two big dogs in here to keep people out.

This is me and Bessie. She's laid her eggs in my billycart, and I can't use it for my paper run. I hope they hurry up and hatch.

PEAR

1928

My name's Bridie and this is my place. I'm seven. I was born in Dublin, but Pa and Mumma left because there wasn't much work there. Now Pa reckons jobs are getting hard to find here too. The rest of my family is Paddy and Declan and Kathleen and now Colum. Mumma says he was a surprise. Pa and Paddy and Declan all work at the brickworks. Dec had to put his age up because he's only thirteen.

I don't have a pet, but Kath and I look after Col in the afternoon because Mumma cleans at the flats. We put him in the pram and bounce him along the creek track till he goes to sleep. I wish the creek was clean enough to swim in.

This is a map of my place. Last year they put in the poles, so now our lights are electric! It's really exciting living here because the aerodrome's just nearby, and sometimes aeroplanes fly over. I climb up the big tree and wave to the pilots. Mumma says we're lucky here because we've got good neighbours. Miss Miller lets Kath and me play her piano, and if we catch Henry's bus he won't let us pay. The Thomsons on the other side have got a wireless! Lorna Thomson's my best friend.

We had a party last Saint Patrick's Day. He's the Saint of Ireland, and we all wear green for him and sing and dance. Pa got a bit sad because he was missing home, so Mumma invited the Next Doors in to cheer him up.

1918

This is my place. Mum calls me Bertie, but Eddie and all the blokes at the hospital call me Champ. I'm nine. My brother Eddie's only got one leg, but he's still great at cricket. He and the blokes sometimes let me play with them down by the creek. I live with Mum and Eddie and my sister Ev, and we let the front room to Miss Walkley, from church. Dad died at Gallipoli. Miss Walkley says that's something to be proud of, but I reckon it stinks. He was a great spin bowler.

This is me and Gert. We got her to help the War Effort.

This is a map of my place. Mum works in the kitchen at the hospital, and when Ev comes home from the factory she puts on her VAD dress and goes over there too. I've got a treehouse in the big tree. Mum says we might have to move to the country because we can't afford to live here now, but I don't want to.

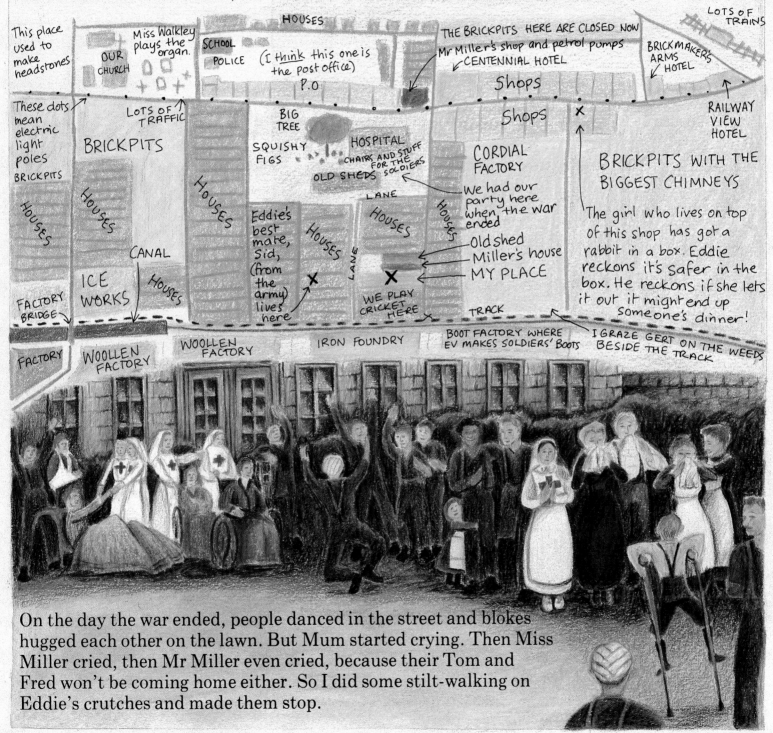

On the day the war ended, people danced in the street and blokes hugged each other on the lawn. But Mum started crying. Then Miss Miller cried, then Mr Miller even cried, because their Tom and Fred won't be coming home either. So I did some stilt-walking on Eddie's crutches and made them stop.

1908

My name's Evelyn and this is my place. I'm ten. We moved here because it's close to the city for Father to get to the bank. Mother teaches music at the college, but of course Eddie and I go to the ordinary school. On the way home, we always wait near the petrol pump on Müllers' corner in case a motor car stops. Father says the main road will be tar soon, and there'll be even more traffic. Of course, Eddie pesters Father about when will we get a motor car, but you'd have to be as rich as anything for that.

This is me and Old Ned. He used to pull a horse bus but Mr Müller put him out to pasture when the trams went electric. He says poor Ned just couldn't keep up.

Last Cracker Night all our street had a bonfire down near the creek. We got crackers from the Chinese shop. Mr Müller said it reminded him of old times.

This is a map of my place. On weekends I play caves under the big tree. Mr Müller says, when he was a boy, a dragon lived across the creek. When I was little I used to believe him.

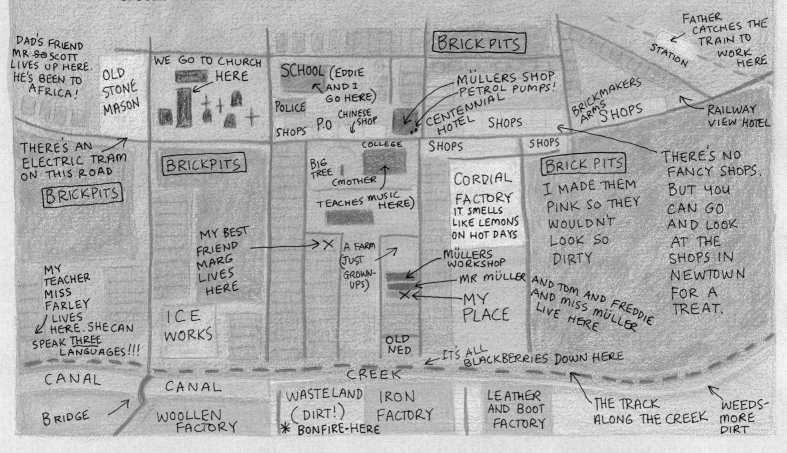

DAD'S FRIEND MR ~~SO~~ SCOTT LIVES UP HERE. HE'S BEEN TO AFRICA!

OLD STONE MASON

WE GO TO CHURCH HERE

SCHOOL (EDDIE AND I GO HERE)

POLICE

SHOPS

P.O

CHINESE SHOP

BRICKPITS

MÜLLERS SHOP PETROL PUMPS!

CENTENNIAL HOTEL   SHOPS

BRICKMAKERS ARMS   SHOPS

STATION

FATHER CATCHES THE TRAIN TO WORK HERE

RAILWAY VIEW HOTEL

THERE'S AN ELECTRIC TRAM ON THIS ROAD

BRICKPITS

BRICKPITS

BRICKPITS

COLLEGE

SHOPS   SHOPS

BIG TREE

(MOTHER TEACHES MUSIC HERE)

CORDIAL FACTORY IT SMELLS LIKE LEMONS ON HOT DAYS

BRICK PITS

I MADE THEM PINK SO THEY WOULDN'T LOOK SO DIRTY

THERE'S NO FANCY SHOPS. BUT YOU CAN GO AND LOOK AT THE SHOPS IN NEWTOWN FOR A TREAT.

MY TEACHER MISS FARLEY LIVES HERE. SHE CAN SPEAK THREE LANGUAGES!!!

MY BEST FRIEND MARG LIVES HERE

X   A FARM (JUST GROWN-UPS)

MÜLLERS WORKSHOP

MR MÜLLER

X   MY PLACE

AND TOM AND FREDDIE AND MISS MÜLLER LIVE HERE

ICE WORKS

OLD NED

IT'S ALL BLACKBERRIES DOWN HERE

CANAL

CANAL

CREEK

THE TRACK ALONG THE CREEK

WEEDS-MORE DIRT

BRIDGE

WOOLLEN FACTORY

WASTELAND (DIRT!) * BONFIRE-HERE

IRON FACTORY

LEATHER AND BOOT FACTORY

1898

This is my place. My name's Rowley. I'm eight. My mum and me, we rent the upstairs front room. Auntie Adie's got the middle room and Miss Singer's got the back. Mum works at the laundry with Auntie Adie. She's not really my auntie, but I call her that. Downstairs, there's Mr Merry. He does photographs, but on weekends he has an icecream cart, and he lets me and Tommy Müller help him. Tom lives next door. His auntie's got a bicycle!

This is a map of my place. The big tree belongs to the posh school, but I climb it anyway. A bit down the creek, it turns into a canal, and there are barges. Before my dad went away, he helped build it. Mum says he just couldn't find any more work, and one day he might come back.

76

STATION

RAILWAY LINE

MORE BRICKPITS

You catch mr Müller's horse bus here

Brickmakers Arms

RAILWAY VIEW HOTEL

Archie reckons there's ghosts here.

SCHOOL

POLICE

Chinese shop

MÜLLERS

P.O.

Centennial Hotel. Tommy and me get mr merry's beer here.

BRICKPITS

There's tracks for the steam tram on this road

The kid here got gastro

All these shops are empty

This is the laundry where Mum and Auntie Adie work.

Archie lives here. He's a bully. He picks on me if I walk down this street!

BRICKPITS

POSH SCHOOL

BIG TREE

POSH KIDS KEEP THEIR CRICKET AND FOOTBALL STUFF HERE

There's a farm I forgot

Müllers workshop.

My mate Tom Müller lives here with his mum and dad and Freddie and their Auntie

My dad used to work here but he got a bad cough and the boss told him to leave.

BRICKPITS

There's some houses here they never finished

Iceworks

The cows for the dairy live here

LANE

My PLACE!

Ned Kelly grazes here

MORE BRICKPITS

CREEK TRACK

CREEK TRACK

CANAL - Dad built this

All weeds and rubbish

Bridge

They're building a new factory here. Maybe my dad can get a job here.

Some sort of ironworks

Vegetable garden

new road

All this is weeds, but sometimes pumpkin comes up all by itself. Yuk, I hate pumpkin.

Once a month, Mr Merry has a party. It's called the Labor Party, and it's just grown-ups sitting in his room and talking. Miss Müller goes, but Mum and Auntie Adie don't. Mr Merry gives Tom and me a shilling to nick up to the pub and bring them back some beer. He lets us keep the change!

This is me and Ned Kelly. He's the front horse on Mr Müller's bus. Mr Müller reckons you've got to be an outlaw, to beat the new trams. I'd like to be a tram driver when I grow up, but most people round here make bricks, so maybe I will too. Mr Merry reckons every brick in every house tells a story.

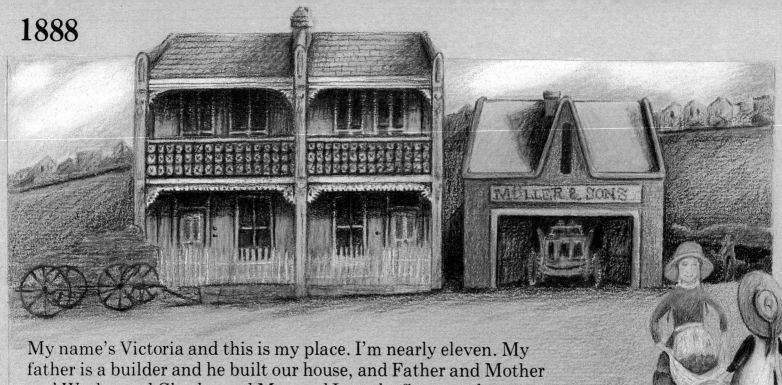

My name's Victoria and this is my place. I'm nearly eleven. My father is a builder and he built our house, and Father and Mother and Wesley and Charles and May and I are the first people ever ever to live here! Father built the next door house too, for the Müllers, and now he's started two more houses on the other side. Our house is the biggest. We've got three bedrooms upstairs, and downstairs there's a parlour and a dining-room, then the breezeway, then the kitchen. We've even got tap water. Mother says it's like a Dream Come True, but sometimes Father looks worried.

This is a map of my place. Mother reckons you get sick if you even look at the creek, but Father says it'll get better soon when they finish making the sewerage. Sometimes I play on the swing in the big tree, but the Owen girls don't talk to me. As if I'd care! The hotel's just changed its name because of the Centenary. Mother won't even let me walk on that side of the road. We're all in the Temperance League.

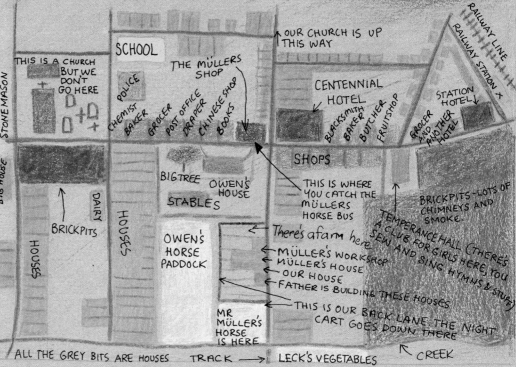

THIS IS A CHURCH BUT WE DON'T GO HERE

SCHOOL

OUR CHURCH IS UP THIS WAY

THE MÜLLERS SHOP

STONE MASON

POLICE

CHEMIST
BAKER
GROCER
POST OFFICE
DRAPER
CHINESE SHOP
BOOKS

CENTENNIAL HOTEL

BLACKSMITH
BAKER
BUTCHER
FRUITSHOP

RAILWAY LINE
RAILWAY STATION X

STATION HOTEL

GROCER AND ANOTHER HOTEL

BIG HOUSE

BIG TREE

OWEN'S HOUSE

STABLES

SHOPS

THIS IS WHERE YOU CATCH THE MÜLLERS HORSE BUS

BRICKPITS—LOTS OF CHIMNEYS AND SMOKE.

HOUSES

DAIRY

BRICKPITS

HOUSES

OWEN'S HORSE PADDOCK

There's a farm here

TEMPERANCE HALL (THERE'S A CLUB FOR GIRLS HERE, YOU SEW AND SING HYMNS & stuff)

MÜLLER'S WORKSHOP
MÜLLER'S HOUSE
OUR HOUSE
FATHER IS BUILDING THESE HOUSES

THIS IS OUR BACK LANE. THE NIGHT CART GOES DOWN THERE

MR MÜLLER'S HORSE IS HERE

ALL THE GREY BITS ARE HOUSES

TRACK →

LECK'S VEGETABLES

CREEK

This year, Australia had its hundredth birthday! We went to the Centennial Picnic with the Müllers, in their horse bus. Miss Müller works in town, at the telephone exchange, and she catches the train to work! Mother says ladies don't have jobs, but I want to be something when I grow up.

This is me and Squarker. Sometimes he gives you a real fright. Once he made the dunny can man drop everything.

1878

This is my place. My name's really Heinrich, but everyone except my grandparents calls me Henry. I'm ten. When my mother died, Minna stopped being a teacher, and she looks after Father and Anna and me. I used to have a little brother too, but he got the gastro. My grandparents and Uncle Wolf live on top of the new shop. My grandfather says that one day I will own it, but I want to be a balloonist.
I didn't tell him that.

MÜLLER & SONS

This is me and Gretchen. She's Minna's cat, but she's mine too.

Stone mason

I go to school here

Church

wheelwright
the new post office
draper
grocer
bootmaker

houses

Our new shop where we sell saddlery. My grandparents live upstairs.

Bay View Hotel

blacksmith
baker
butcher
grocer

There are gas lights all along the road now.

Brickmaker's Arms

big house

BRICKYARD

Big tree

Roses

The Owens live here

Mr Owen has sold this. There's going to be shops.

The carter's yard

brickpits

Chimneys

DAIRY

More cows

Stables

a little farm

The people here look after the cows

Big workshop where we make saddles and harnesses.

Mr Owen's horses

Our house

my grandfather has bought our land from Mr Owen.

Well

Cows—but my father says this will be sold soon.

They're starting to build houses here

This is the creek. It smells.

stepping stones
this is where I saw the dragon

Bridge

This is where our vegetables come from.

This is a map of my place. I get over the fence and climb the big tree and pretend I'm on a balloon. The creek's so dirty, Minna won't let me play in it. She says it's like an open sewer, and that's why my brother Siggie died.

One night I woke up and there was all this banging and yelling. I crept out into the street and it was coming from Mr Wong's garden. So I went across the stepping stones, and there was a dragon!

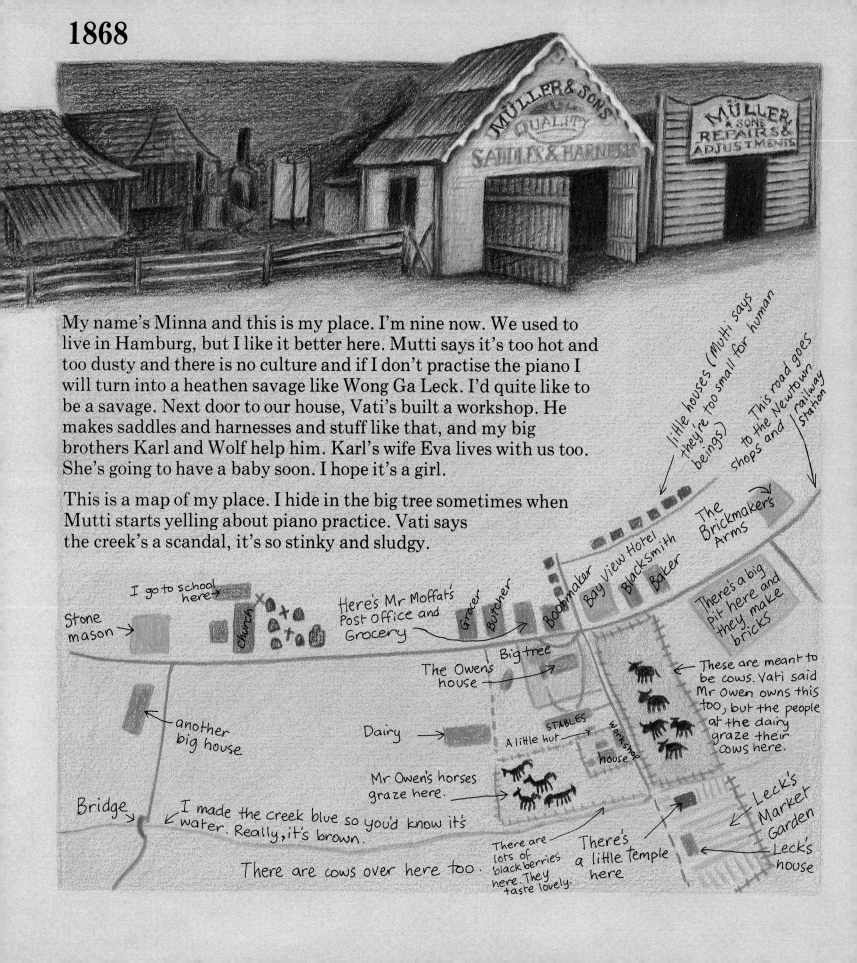

1868

My name's Minna and this is my place. I'm nine now. We used to live in Hamburg, but I like it better here. Mutti says it's too hot and too dusty and there is no culture and if I don't practise the piano I will turn into a heathen savage like Wong Ga Leck. I'd quite like to be a savage. Next door to our house, Vati's built a workshop. He makes saddles and harnesses and stuff like that, and my big brothers Karl and Wolf help him. Karl's wife Eva lives with us too. She's going to have a baby soon. I hope it's a girl.

This is a map of my place. I hide in the big tree sometimes when Mutti starts yelling about piano practice. Vati says the creek's a scandal, it's so stinky and sludgy.

little houses (Mutti says they're too small for human beings)

This road goes to the Newtown shops and railway station

The Brickmaker's Arms

Bay View Hotel
Blacksmith
Baker

There's a big pit here and they make bricks

I go to school here→

Church

Stone mason →

Here's Mr Moffat's Post Office and Grocery

Grocer
Butcher
Bootmaker

Big tree

The Owen's house →

These are meant to be cows. Vati said Mr Owen owns this too, but the people at the dairy graze their cows here.

another big house

Dairy →

A little hut →

STABLES

workshop
house

Mr Owen's horses graze here. →

Bridge →

I made the creek blue so you'd know it's water. Really, it's brown.

There are cows over here too.

There are lots of blackberries here. They taste lovely.

There's a little temple here

Leck's Market Garden

Leck's house

At Christmas time, we have a
proper German party, with a fir
tree and candles. Then we sing
around the piano. It still seems
funny, without any snow. But the
food tastes just as good.

This is me and my kitten
Gretchen. Leck gave her to me.
Some of the other kids chase after
Leck and pull his pigtail, but he's
my friend.

1858

This is my place. My name's Benjamin Franklin and I am twelve years old. I was born in San Francisco but Mother says Dad got Gold Fever. First we went to the Californian fields, but he didn't find anything, so we moved to Australia and he tried his luck out Bathurst way. And when that was no good, we moved here. Now Dad works for Mr Moffatt, but I don't think he likes it.

Last Thanksgiving, Mother cooked a turkey like she used to do at home. Sometimes I wish I wasn't American, because the other kids laugh at how I speak, but Dad says one day everyone in the world will be free and equal and like brothers and sisters. When I think how Beth and Amy and I fight, I don't reckon it'll be much different.

This is Tripod. I share her with Leck. We found her one day down the back of the joss house. The other kids tease Leckie too, so we stick together.

This is a map of my place. The creek's too dirty to swim in, but Leck and I make boats and race them down it. Sometimes we hide up the big tree and throw the figs down at the kids who call us things.

Inn

Minister's house

I go to school here Leckie doesn't.

Church

cemetery

Druggist

Butcher's shop

Mr Moffat's grocery · Dad works here.

farrier

Houses

BAY VIEW HOTEL

There's a railway station up at Newtown now. It takes about twenty minutes to walk there if you go really fast.

Dr Cheadle's house

There's a big hole here

big tree

Stables and coach yard

Posh House. The Owens live here It's like a castle!!

My Place Dad rents it from the Owens

Bridge

The Creek
(Amy fell in and Leckie got her out)

Some old orange trees

down this way there's the river

stepping stones

Leck's house

Joss House (Leckie's church)

market garden

Swampy land— lots of birds and tadpoles.

There's factories and stuff over here ↓

track →

1848

My name's Johanna and this is my place. Soon I'll be ten. I live here with Granny Sarah because my ma died when she had me. She was called Alice. Granny Sarah grows vegetables, and I help her carry them around to people's houses and sell them. We use creek water for the garden, but you can't drink it. There's a woolwashery up near the swamp and they drain all their yuk into our creek!

This is a map of my place. Sometimes I creep into the Owens' garden and climb the big tree. If Mr Owen catches me, he gives me a weird look, but he just stomps away. Granny Sarah says I'm never to go there.

Last time Uncle Sam came home, we had a party. He's a sailor, and you'd never guess what he brought me! Auntie Maryann got a half-holiday. She's Mrs Owen's upstairs maid. Uncle Davey still lived here then, but he's gone out Bathurst way now to be a shepherd for Mr Charles, and Granny Sarah says that one day we might move there too. She reckons too many people live here now, and she's fed to the teeth with the dust of the main road and all the traffic.

This is me and Mischief. Isn't he beautiful!

This is my place. I'm Davey, and I'm seven. Just Ma and me live here now, because Alice and Maryann live up at the new house and are maids. Sam's my brother, but he's on a ship catching whales. He's fourteen.

Before Sam went away, Mr Owen was shot by bushrangers, so Mr John became the master. Ma says he's even worse. Mr John's sold most of the farm, and there are three more big houses now between here and the river.

This is a map of my place. When the wind blows the wrong way, it stinks from Mr John's tannery. Ma says we're really lucky we're up the good end of the creek, but she won't eat the oysters any more. There's a swing in the big tree for Mr John's kids and I'm not allowed to play on it. So I climb up and drop figs on them, and they run away. Once Mr John caught me and whipped me, but it was worth it. They're snobs.

lime kilns

There is a new dam here with a bridge across the top

← Mr Owen was shot up this way.

Road- lots of people drive along here from Sydney to go for picnics by the river

Inn

BIG house

little houses (fishermen and lime workers)

WATER

CREEK

The Owen's tannery and woollen mill are down this way

When I was little, my father fell off the roof of the new house and died. Ma says she hates the Owens and all their works. I don't really remember him, but one night last summer Ma took me to the creek and lit a big campfire. We stayed up all night, and she told me how Dad discovered the swimming hole!

This is the new church. My dad is buried here.

There's a horse trough here now

Brady's Inn

To New Town then to Sydney

Little farms and houses

X = My Place

✝ = Church is being built here

= big tree

● = New House (Owens)

= Mr John Owen has kept this land

= Mr Owen used to own all this and more, but after he died Mr John divided it up and sold it.

● = This is the swimming hole my dad found.

This is all swampy land (no fish but lots of frogs!)

you can cross the creek here

This is me and Duchess. She belongs to Mr John, but the groom lets me brush her. Next year I'm starting work as a stable boy.

1828

My name's Alice and this is my place. I'm nine and a quarter. Another girl called Alice lived here once, but she died, and Ma gave me her name. The Owens used to live here, but they're staying in Sydney Town till their new house is built. Mr John still often comes back to check on things. Ma and Dad live here too of course, and Maryann and Little Sam. Dad's in charge of the farm and the convicts. They're making a quarry to get stone for the new house. I take them their lunch.

This is me and Wilhemina. She loves it when I scratch her back.

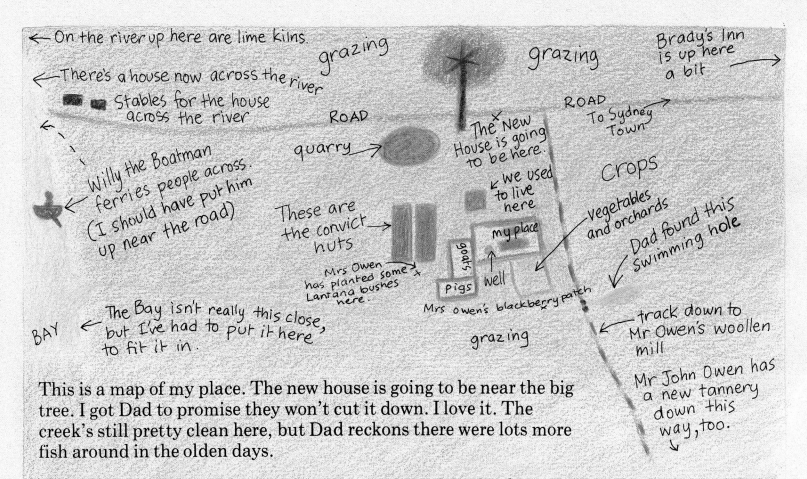

← On the river up here are lime kilns.

grazing   grazing   Brady's Inn is up here a bit →

← There's a house now across the river

Stables for the house across the river

ROAD   ROAD To Sydney Town →

Willy the Boatman ferries people across. (I should have put him up near the road)

quarry →

The New House is going to be here.

← We used to live here

Crops

These are the convict huts →

Vegetables and orchards

Dad found this swimming hole

my place

Mrs Owen has planted some Lantana bushes here.

goats

Pigs   well

Mrs Owen's blackberry patch

track down to Mr Owen's woollen mill

BAY ← The Bay isn't really this close, but I've had to put it here, to fit it in.

grazing

Mr John Owen has a new tannery down this way, too.

This is a map of my place. The new house is going to be near the big tree. I got Dad to promise they won't cut it down. I love it. The creek's still pretty clean here, but Dad reckons there were lots more fish around in the olden days.

The night the Owens went, we all had a party. Dad used to be a convict too, so he doesn't treat the men like slaves, like Mr Owen and Mr John do. Ma roasted a whole sheep, and Old Freddie danced on the table.

1818

This is my place. My name's Charles and I'm eight and a half. I live here with my mother and my brother John and my sister Meg, and sometimes my father. I had another sister called Alice but she died. Sam and Sarah are our servants. Sam is in charge of things because Father is mostly in Sydney. John says Father is making money. He's got a new woollen mill across the swamp. John says he's going to make money too when he grows up, but I want to be a farmer.

This is me and Daisy. Sarah taught me to milk her. Sarah's nice. She lets me turn the handle on the butter-churn, and drink the buttermilk.

When Sam and Sarah got married, we had a party. Mother lent Sarah her second best shawl and Father gave them a guinea and three days' holiday. John got drunk on rum.

This is a map of my place. The long hut up the back is for the convicts. Mother says I'm not allowed to talk to them, but I do. The big tree is great to climb. When I'm up the top I pretend I've crossed the Blue Mountains, and I'm choosing some land for my very own farm. The other good thing is the creek. I build dams, but John breaks them up.

1808

My name's Sarah and this is my place. I'm nine. I was born in Sydney but my mother came from England on a convict ship. Last year she died so Mrs Owen took me as a servant. She doesn't beat me much, but you should see all the work I have to do! Mrs Owen lives here too of course, and Alice and the baby John. Mr Owen's mainly in Sydney, doing business. Mrs Owen runs the farm, and she has five convict servants and Sam to help her. Sam used to be a convict but now he's a ticket-of-leave man. He's more like my family than anyone else in the world.

This is me and Pokey. I call her that because she pokes her head into my lean-to at night. I steal crusts for her, and she's learning to eat from my hand. She's my secret.

One day, some soldiers came to see Mr Owen. They ate and drank a lot, and talked about kicking out Governor Bligh. I hate it when adults get drunk and talk politics, so I nicked some jam roly and some oranges, and Alice and I went up to the big tree and had our own party.

This is a map of my place. I look after the vegetables, and they taste great. The wheat and stuff all goes to Sydney. Sam swims in a deep hole in the creek but I'm not allowed to.

This is my place. My name's Sam, and I was born in London. I'm eleven. The judge put me in gaol because I stole a jacket. I was cold. In the gaol they beat me. Then they put me on a ship and sent me here. Then they let me out to work for Mr Owen. Sometimes he whips me too. But at least it's not cold, and I can catch heaps of fish to eat.

Last Christmas, Mr Owen gave me a holiday. Mrs Owen is still in England and she sent out a pudding. Mr Owen drank a lot of rum and let me eat as much as I liked. I've never had a pudding or a holiday before.

This is me and Katie. I milk her every morning, and at night I put her in the pen in case the blacks get her.

This is a map of my place. We're clearing the bush back to make a farm. It gives me blisters. Mr Owen has 90 acres, but he wants to buy more. I think he's got too much already. Sometimes he goes off to Sydney Cove to get supplies, and doesn't come back for a week. I get scared at night then, but in the daytime I nick down the creek. I've found a great swimming hole.

At the top of the hill there's a big tree. I climb up it and pretend I can see all the way to Shoreditch. That's where my mother is, and my sisters and brother. I wish I had someone to play with.

1788

My name's Barangaroo. I belong to this place. We're staying here for the summer, at the creek camp, to get the fish down in the bay. But often we stay a while at other places. Everywhere we go is home. I live with my parents and my brother Bereewan and my grandparents and my aunties and uncles and cousins. We take our tools and our hunting and fishing stuff with us when we move, but of course we leave the huts and canoes here for next time. Sometimes I wonder what it would be like to stop in the same place always, but my grandmother says no one does that. I guess it would be boring.

This is a map of this place. We camp here because the creek water's so fresh and good, and we're close to the river and the bay. In the creek there's a great swimming hole where my cousins and I always play. My father says he swam in exactly the same place when he was a boy, and my grandfather says he did too. At the top of the hill there's a big fig tree.

The RIVER

We fish up the river too

My father and the other men go up this way to get kangaroo.

big tree on hill

the huts

there are big stepping stones here

Mangrove trees

The fires keep the mossies away.

The Bay

there's heaps of fish

mud flats good oysters

good crabs

the creek

Swampy land

Swimming hole

We keep the canoes here. We all go out fishing in the bay.

This is our dog. He sleeps with me.

Last week a whale got washed up on the bay, so we invited some other people from round about, and had a big barbecue. As well as the meat, we had piles of vegetables, and oysters and pippies and crabs and octopus and I've forgotten what else. I ate so much I thought I'd explode. Then I fell asleep till the night-time party started.

Sometimes, at the end of the day, I climb to the top of the big tree and play that I'm the only person in the world. If I look one way, the sea runs out till it meets the sky. But the other way, the land goes on till the sun sets.

My grandmother says, 'We've always belonged to this place.'

'But how long?' I ask. 'And how far?'

My grandmother says, 'For ever and ever.'

Acknowledgements

We'd like to thank all the people who
helped us do the research for this book,
especially Carol Allport, Chrys Meader,
Fred McCarthy and Annie Ross. Thanks
too to Collins Dove, for believing in us and our
ideas, and to Gay, for enthusiastic
typesetting. Finally, thanks to
David and Ken, for being sounding
boards and life support systems.